20 Articles FROM 20 Years

Timeless Selections

FROM THE

Responsive Classroom® Newsletter

The stories in this book are all based on real events in the classroom. However, in order to respect the privacy of students, names and many identifying characteristics of students and situations have been changed.

ISBN: 978-1-892989-26-0

Library of Congress Control Number: 2008923955

Editor: Alice Yang
Photographs: Jeff Woodward and Peter Wrenn, unless otherwise noted.
Cover and book design: Helen Merena

Northeast Foundation for Children, Inc.
85 Avenue A, Suite 204
P. O. Box 718
Turners Falls, MA 01376-0718

800-360-6332
www.responsiveclassroom.org

12 11 10 09 08   6 5 4 3 2 1

We would like to thank Sharon Dunn for the
countless volunteer hours she has devoted to the
creation and ongoing development of the
Responsive Classroom Newsletter.

Her vision provided the inspiration; her practical
guidance got the newsletter off the ground
and helped to sustain it for twenty years.

TABLE OF CONTENTS

Working with Families

Managing Challenging Behaviors

20 Articles
FROM 20 Years

Timeless Selections

FROM THE

Responsive Classroom® Newsletter

INTRODUCTION

by Jay Lord, NEFC co-founder

This book celebrates twenty years of publication of the *Responsive Classroom Newsletter*, 1989–2008. This flagship periodical of Northeast Foundation for Children (NEFC) is and has always been a newsletter for teachers by teachers. It is filled with practical strategies and stories from elementary teachers that inspire, instruct, and invigorate fellow teachers in building the potential of each and every child. Collected here are twenty timeless articles from these two decades.

Along with the celebration of the newsletter, this book also celebrates the rich history of NEFC and the pedagogy it developed: the *Responsive Classroom* approach for fostering social, emotional, and academic growth in a strong and safe school community.

NEFC was created in 1981, eight years before the inception of the newsletter. In Franklin County, Massachusetts, a group of teachers collaboratively founded Northeast Foundation for Children and the Greenfield Center School. These teachers, riled by the state of public education, wanted to be part of the conversation on school reform right from the steps of their school house.

Greenfield Center School was to be their laboratory, NEFC their conduit to public school teachers. Teaching strategies developed and tested at the school would be shared with other educators through workshops and publications offered by NEFC. The school opened with sixty children and four teachers; NEFC opened with possibility.

※

Fast forward to 1989. Greenfield Center School has been successful and is growing. NEFC has just begun to offer professional development workshops. This year it is offering a week-long workshop in two locations, New York State and New Hampshire. The organization recently published its first book, *A Notebook for Teachers: Making Changes in the Elementary Curriculum*, and just released its first video, *Places to Start: Implementing the Developmental Classroom*.

Now NEFC sees the need for a way to share *Responsive Classroom* ideas regularly with teachers in a free, convenient format. Thus the newsletter is born. The first issue goes out to 5,000 subscribers.

This first issue leads with an article by Chip Wood, co-founder of NEFC. It decries the trend to push formalized textbook, workbook, and paper-and-pencil academics down onto younger and younger children, even kindergartners, at the expense of developmentally appropriate play. Wood writes,

> "But," [teachers] ask. "What can I do? I'm only one teacher. How can I make a difference?"

Wood answers that teachers can make a difference by advocating for change. Teachers can talk to school boards, administrators, parents, and educational publishers, telling them no more paper-and-pencil before children are ready and inviting them to visit classrooms with developmentally appropriate hands-on activities to see the rich learning taking place. In this way, Wood writes, teachers can "return the classroom to the children and teaching to the teacher." Teachers, he asserts, are the difference makers.

※

Fast forward again to 1993. Greenfield Center School is flourishing. NEFC has published four books and is offering more professional development workshops. It has just begun fulfilling its first major consulting contract, helping teachers in a large urban school district learn to use the *Responsive Classroom* approach.

The November issue of the newsletter again leads with an article by Chip Wood, this one about the various forms of violence children experience at school and outside of school. The headline reads,

Our Violent Culture: Can Teachers Make a Difference?

Yes, we can, Wood answers, by making caring part of every curriculum. We can teach the skills that lead children to behave in caring ways. Teaching caring in the classroom is not a total solution, he says, "but it is something we can do, and we can do it now."

That article, and articles from other installments of the newsletter, go on to suggest specific ways to teach caring—through *Responsive Classroom* Morning Meeting, through engaging children in creating and living their classroom rules, through teaching children to use materials creatively and responsibly, through teaching children to give compliments and constructive critiques and to ask for and give help. Issue after issue, the newsletter is adding to each teacher's toolbox of concrete strategies for teaching children to care and for helping them to succeed.

※

It is now 2008. We are in our twentieth year of publication of the newsletter. Many things have changed. NEFC has published thirty titles and offers *Responsive Classroom* week-long workshops at thirty-six sites throughout the country. It trains 6,000

2

teachers a year in week-long workshops and annually sells books about classroom practice to more than 100,000 teachers, who teach more than 2,000,000 children. Greenfield Center School and NEFC have become two separate organizations so that each may better serve its constituents.

Coming with this growth has been a broadening of the *Responsive Classroom* pedagogy and a diversification of the people behind it. The approach began as a way to teach specific content areas in developmentally appropriate ways. Now it focuses on ten key classroom practices that integrate social, academic, and emotional learning. Together, the practices offer a comprehensive approach to classroom management and instructional delivery.

As NEFC and the *Responsive Classroom* approach have evolved, so has the newsletter. It now goes out to 70,000 teachers four times a year. Whereas in the early days the articles were written by a handful of founders and in-house staff, now they are authored by teacher contributors from all over the country. The current breadth of topics also reflects the expanded *Responsive Classroom* pedagogy.

NEFC no longer dwells in mere possibility; it has realized many of its early ambitions and is beginning to imagine more. It has moved from a mom and pop corner store to a proud institution with a rich tradition.

But these twenty years are also a testimony to the fact that the more things change, the more they stay the same. Through all the evolution and all the expansion, one belief remains constant. We still hold with deep conviction that teachers do make a difference, that good teachers, through everyday interactions with children, can stretch children's potential and help them achieve things they never thought possible.

In their 2008 article, "Getting Past 'I Can't'," Andy Dousis and Roxann Kriete tell about teaching children to persevere when they get stumped by hard academics or any kind of challenge.★ The story centers on one fourth grade child struggling with two-digit multiplication in Dousis's class. Dousis says,

> I knew I had an opportunity here to help one child
> get one step closer to [seeing] herself as a learner. My
> task was to teach perseverance. Perseverance ... is not
> simply a character trait that some have and others do
> not. I believe that like multiplication, classification,
> and long division, perseverance can be taught, not by
> stirring speeches or inspirational posters on the wall,
> but in the ordinary, everyday encounters that class-
> room life offers in abundance.

★ *This article was published after this book's manuscript was finalized. Go to www.responsiveclassroom.org/newsletter/ 20_1nl_1.html to read the article.*

＊

The power of teaching, as Dousis and Kriete assert, is mainly in the ordinary: The routine and pace of our day makes or breaks children; the words we use can build up children's confidence or bring it down; the methods we adopt can lead children to gain competence or stall out.

The work of teaching is in the detail, and in the detail is where the *Responsive Classroom Newsletter* dwells. An enduring hallmark of the newsletter's articles is their practicality. They offer use-it-tomorrow suggestions for managing the nuts and bolts of elementary classroom and school life. Some of the practical ideas you'll find in this collection of twenty articles are for:

* Welcoming children to school in the morning

* Bringing closure at the end of the day

* Using open-ended questions to stretch children's academic and social learning

* Teaching lunch and recess so that these are productive and peaceful times of the day

* Inviting parents into the classroom community

* Problem-solving with students

* Teaching children with challenging behaviors

We invite you to explore, skip around, or dawdle in reading this book. We hope that by the end you'll see why we believe so strongly that "Yes, we as teachers can make a difference. And yes, we as teachers must make a difference."

We hope you will also have gained some ideas for *how* teachers can make a difference. As the *Responsive Classroom Newsletter* embarks on its next twenty years, we continue to ask these important "how" questions: "How can we as teachers, with intention and consistency, better stretch children toward their potential? How can we as teachers help all children take better care of themselves, each other, and the world they live in?" These are powerful questions, and they are alive and relevant today. With this modest book of twenty articles, we invite you to join the conversation.

Building the Classroom Community

Activities for Building Community in Your Classroom

BY MARLYNN K. CLAYTON

*R*esponsive Classroom teachers begin their school year with curriculum activities that build students' academic skills while creating a sense of community and class identity.

These curriculum activities require children to plan; solve problems; express themselves in many different ways and media; use their writing, reading, and math skills; and actively listen. They help children develop important social skills such as cooperation, assertion, responsibility, empathy, and self-control.

They also provide critical opportunities for children to learn each other's names, interests, and abilities; to feel a sense of belonging; and to invest in caring about a group of people. The following are just a few activities that *Responsive Classroom* teachers have used successfully in many different settings and grade levels.

"Getting to Know One Another" Projects

NAMES

On the first day of school, students make name tags and decorate them in a way that tells something about themselves. Children show their name tags to the rest of the class, talk about them, and then wear them for at least the next ten days. Some teachers have children make the name tags in duplicate so that one set can be used throughout the year for activities that require the drawing of names. Here are some other possible name-related activities after the children have made name tags:

* What's in a name? During the first few days of school, each child shares special information about his or her name. Does it have a meaning? Where did it come from? Does the child prefer a shortened form of the name or a nickname?

* "Names" bulletin board: Children make a bulletin board display with their name tags or with large writing in paint or markers.

* Name posters: Each child creates a name poster with large letters going down the left-hand side and descriptors about them going horizontally out from each letter.

Smart
Awesome
Mighty

Once children know each other, they can make a name poster for another class member.

AUTOBIOGRAPHIES

Children dictate, write, or draw autobiographies, depending on their age and abilities. The teacher can provide blank pages with prompting questions for the children to answer in words or drawings, or a combination of both. Later, pages with children's questions can be added. These books include a self-portrait and sometimes photographs taken at school and/or at home. Teachers can engage children in a wide range of activities using these autobiographies:

* *Read aloud:* Children read their autobiographies aloud to the class.

* *Class library:* Children add their autobiographies to the class library.

* *Who am I?* Teams of children prepare bio sketches based on information gathered from the autobiographies. Each team presents its sketch orally or through drama to the rest of the class, who try to guess the classmate being described.

* *Class riddles:* The teacher, and later the children, prepare "guess the classmate" riddles using information from the autobiographies. The riddles are written on the morning message or presented at Morning Meeting. They can be collected and compiled into a book for continued enjoyment.

* *Bingo:* The teacher makes a bingo grid. Each square contains information that applies to several or many of the children in the class (has a brother, went to the beach for vacation, ate spaghetti this week, etc.). Each child gets a copy of the grid. The children walk around, asking each other questions and crossing out a square when the information applies to the child asked. Children may ask each classmate only one question, then must move on to another child before coming back to the first child. The object is to get three or four in a row or fill in a whole sheet (whatever rules have been established before starting).

* *Pride Day:* Children write or dictate about a skill or hobby that they are proud of, describing how they developed the skill or hobby and why it makes them proud. Then each child has a scheduled day to share this information with the class, perhaps including demonstrating the activity. Students' writings are displayed on a bulletin board or collected into a book, along with any photos of their sharing.

> Spending the time to build community and help children learn about each other's lives sets the foundation for a caring classroom.

INTERVIEWS

Children pair up with classmates they do not know very well, and the partners interview each other, using questions devised jointly by the teacher and students. Children can write up their interviews or record them on video or audio. The final products can include a portrait, clay statue, drama, song, or poem about the partner. As the year goes on, children might interview new partners, perhaps using new questions. These interviews can spawn further community-building activities such as these:

9

* *Display:* The class creates a display of their interviews, complete with photos, clay statues, and other visual representations of their partner.

* *Presentations to the class:* Partners give presentations to the class to share what they learned about each other.

* *Name that Classmate:* The class plays a game similar to Twenty Questions.

  Variation 1: One child has the name of a classmate taped to his or her back. With information from the interviews in mind, the child asks yes/no questions and the class answers (thumbs up for yes, thumbs down for no) until the child guesses the student or reaches twenty questions.

  Variation 2: A child whispers the name of a classmate to one other person. The class asks yes/no questions for the child to answer until they can guess the name or twenty questions are asked.

  Variation 3: Every student has the name of a different classmate taped to his or her back. All students walk around asking and answering yes/no questions to guess the name on their back.

* *Partner project:* Partners interview each other to find out ways they are alike and different and plan a project (song, skit, poem, drawing, etc.) that would show this information. This could turn into a whole class project, too.

SURVEYS

Children identify categories of personal and family characteristics and interests (have only sisters, have only brothers, have no siblings, speak more than one language, have pets, etc.) and carry out surveys to determine class statistics. The class can then use the survey data for a variety of other activities. For example:

* *Graphing:* Students graph the statistics, analyze the data, and write about them.

* *Theme books:* Students create theme books based on the data—"Our Favorite Pets," "Our Siblings," etc.

* *Games:* Children play Bingo, Name that Classmate, and other games using information they learned about individual classmates while conducting the surveys.

* *Class predictions:* As the class thinks of a new survey to conduct, they make predictions about its findings based on past survey information.

Several times a week the class has "new friends" time, when children pair up with classmates they don't know very well to do an activity. These "new friends" times may include:

* Morning Meeting time, when the children sit next to their new friends

* lunch time, when each child eats with a new friend

* choice or activity time, when the children work on an activity with their partners

* game time, when the children play a board game or outdoor game with their new friends

After each "new friends" time, a few children each share something they have in common with their new friend or a fact that they learned about their new friend.

Art Projects

Art projects provide ample opportunities for community building. Here are just a few ideas:

* *Puzzle piece mural:* A large sheet of mural paper is cut into puzzle pieces. Each child gets one piece on which to name and describe or illustrate something that she or he is good at and can be counted on to do to help others in the class (good with math, good at fixing things, good with helping hurt feelings, good at tying shoes, etc.). Throughout the year the teacher helps students make use of each other's competencies.

* *Handprint or footprint mural:* Each child puts his/her name and handprint or footprint on a mural, along with a thought about how he/she will help to make the classroom a friendly place ("I hope to use kind words," "I will try to listen," etc.).

* *Friendship quilt:* Children create a quilt-like mural out of paper or cloth, or they make a real quilt. Each child decorates a square or puts a photo on it.

To take it a step further, the children can each add a unique or interesting piece of biographical information ("2/29" for being born on Leap Day, a flag symbolizing an ethnic heritage, etc.) or something that makes the class special to her or him (a picture of a basketball for hoping to play a lot of basketball with classmates, a picture of a bus for the first year riding a school bus, etc.).

* *"Children, Children, Whom Do You See?"* This is wonderful to do with children in primary grades. The class reads Bill Martin's *Brown Bear, Brown Bear, What Do You See?* Based on that story, they create a book that names every child in the class and has a photograph or portrait of every child.

Creating Excitement for Learning

Spending the time to build community and help children learn about various facets of each other's lives sets the foundation for a caring classroom. It leads children to feel competent and excited to meet learning challenges. It also establishes the notion that learning can be fun. So be creative, let the children join in, and enjoy those first few weeks!

———————————————

Editor's note: To learn more strategies for building community at the beginning of the year, see *The First Six Weeks of School* by Paula Denton and Roxann Kriete, published by Northeast Foundation for Children.

Morning Meeting
A Powerful Way to Begin the Day

AN ADAPTED EXCERPT FROM
THE MORNING MEETING BOOK BY ROXANN KRIETE

In the spring of my first year as a secondary school teacher, I got a letter from a student for whom I had a particular fondness, letting me know that she was dropping out of school. School wasn't making much sense to her, and little that she was being asked to learn held much interest for her.

She wrote, almost apologetically, that school just wasn't a place she felt she belonged. More than twenty years later, her words still seem profoundly sad to me:

I will always remember how you said "Hi, Sue" as I walked into eighth period. It made me feel like it really mattered that I came.

It touched and pained me that something which seemed so small to me, an act I hadn't even been aware of, had meant so much to her. I vowed to learn something from it and became more intentional about greeting my students.

I stationed myself by the door and tried to say a little something to each one as the children entered, or at least to make eye contact and smile at every student, not just the ones like Sue for whom I had an instinctive affinity.

13

Gradually I realized how much I was learning at my post by the door. I observed who bounced in with head up and smile wide, whose eyes were red-rimmed from tears shed in the girls' room at lunch, who mumbled a response into his collar and averted his eyes every day for an entire semester. I didn't know what to do about much of it, but at least I was learning how to notice.

I have learned a lot since then. It is good for students to be noticed, to be seen by their teacher. But it is only a start, not enough by itself. They must notice and be noticed by each other as well.

Years after I taught Sue, I joined the staff of Greenfield Center School, Northeast Foundation for Children's K–8 lab school. There, I saw teachers teaching students to greet each other, to speak to each other, to listen to each other. I saw students start each day together in Morning Meeting, where noticing and being noticed were explicit goals.

Today, many children in kindergartens and elementary and middle schools around the country launch their school days in Morning Meetings. All classroom members—grown-ups and students—gather in a circle, greet each other, listen and respond to each other's news, practice academic and social skills, and look forward to the events in the day ahead. Morning Meeting is a particular and deliberate way to begin the day, a way which builds a community of caring and motivated learners.

The Format

Morning Meeting is made up of four sequential components and lasts up to a total of a half hour each day. The components provide daily opportunities for children to practice the skills of greeting, listening and responding, speaking to a group, reading, group problem-solving, and noticing and anticipating. The four components are:

* Greeting—Children greet each other by name, often including handshaking, clapping, singing, and other activities.

* Sharing—Students share some news of interest to the class and respond to each other, articulating their thoughts, feelings, and ideas in a positive manner.

* Group Activity—The whole class does a short activity together, building class cohesion through active participation.

* Morning Message—Students develop language skills and learn about the events in the day ahead by reading and discussing a daily message posted for them.

Teachers and students crave a certain amount of predictability and routine in the school day, especially at the start. The format of Morning Meeting is predictable, but there is plenty of room for variation and change. Meetings reflect the style and flavor of individual teachers and groups. They also reflect the ebb and flow of a school year's seasons—September's new shoes and anxious, careful faces; December's pre-holiday excitement; February's endless runny noses; April's spring-has-sprung exuberance. Its mixture of routine and surprise, of comfort and challenge, make Morning Meeting a treasured and flexible teaching tool.

Morning Meeting Sets the Tone for Learning

The way we begin each day in our classroom sets the tone for learning and speaks volumes about what and whom we value, about our expectations for the way we will treat each other, and about the way we believe learning occurs.

Children's learning begins the second they walk in the doors of the building. It matters to children whether they are greeted warmly or overlooked, whether the classroom feels chaotic and unpredictable, or ordered and comforting. If they announce, "My cat got hit by a car last night but it's gonna be all right," they may find an interested, supportive audience or one that turns away. Every detail of their experience informs students about their classroom and their place in it.

When we start the day with everyone together, face-to-face, welcoming each person, sharing news, listening to individual voices, and communicating as a caring group, we make several powerful statements. We say that every person matters. We say that the way we interact individually and as a group matters. We say that our culture is one of friendliness and thoughtfulness. We say that hard work can be accomplished and important discoveries can be made by playing together. We say that teachers hold authority, even though they are a part of the circle. We say that this is a place where courtesy and warmth and safety reign.

In order to learn, we must take risks—offering up a tentative answer we are far from sure is right or trying out a new part in the choir when we are not sure we can hit the notes. We can take these risks only when we know we will be respected and valued, no matter the outcome. We must trust in order to risk, and Morning Meeting helps create a climate of trust.

> Researchers are now confirming that social skills ... are inextricably intertwined with cognitive growth and intellectual progress.

Morning Meeting Merges Social and Academic Learning

Morning Meeting provides an arena where distinctions that define social, emotional, and academic skills fade and learning becomes an integrated experience.

Teachers have long known and researchers are now confirming that social skills are not just something to be taught so that children behave well enough to get on with the real business of schooling. Rather, they are inextricably intertwined with cognitive growth and intellectual progress. A person who can listen well, who can frame a good question and has the assertiveness to pose it, and who can examine a situation from a number of perspectives will be a strong learner.

All those skills—skills essential to academic achievement—must be modeled, experienced, practiced, extended, and refined in the context of social interaction. Morning Meeting is a forum in which all that happens. It is not an add-on, something extra to make time for, but rather an integral part of the day's planning and curriculum.

A Microcosm of the Way We Wish Our Schools to Be

The time one commits to Morning Meeting is an investment which is repaid many times over. The sense of group belonging and the skills of attention, listening, expression, and cooperative interaction developed in Morning Meeting are a foundation for every lesson, every transition time, every lining-up, every upset and conflict, all day and all year long. Morning Meeting is a microcosm of the way we wish our schools to be—communities full of learning, safe and respectful and challenging for all.

Closing Meeting
Creating a Peaceful End to the School Day

BY CAROL DAVIS

It's 3:23 and my class has just finished a science experiment. I look at the clock and realize we have seven minutes to clean up from science and do everything else we need to do to walk out the door at 3:30 to go home. "Okay, class, we have seven minutes until the bell rings. You need to stop what you're doing, clean up, and get yourself ready to go home. We'll talk about what you discovered from your science experiment tomorrow. Let's hurry. We now only have six minutes. Go!"

They're off! Twenty-eight children are moving in all directions. They scurry around the room putting the science equipment back on the science table, cleaning up their workspaces, washing their hands at the sink, and throwing away trash in the wastebasket.

At the same time, I'm collecting everyone's science observation journals while being the constant watcher of the clock. "We have three minutes! You should be starting to pack up your things to go home. Hurry! Hurry!"

The children shift gears and begin collecting book bags, coats, and lunchboxes. Meanwhile, several children are mindful that they have class jobs to complete before they go home. They begin passing out papers that need to go home, washing the boards, and feeding the class rabbit. I'm trying to figure out who's supposed to stay after school for a Girl Scout meeting, reminding John not to ride the bus because his mom is picking him up for a doctor's appointment, making sure everyone has the right chapter book to read at home, while directing children to stack their chairs and line up.

In the midst of all the chaos, the PA system is blaring with the afternoon announcements that no one can hear. The bell rings and the children exit feeling rushed and unsettled. I feel exhausted.

We Needed a Change

This was how most days ended during my early teaching years until one year I decided that something had to change. I was taking so much care every day to plan and facilitate a Morning Meeting to build community and set a positive tone for the day to come. I realized that it was just as important to take the same care in creating a good ending to our day.

I talked to my class one afternoon. They agreed that the way school ended was frustrating and chaotic. We were all tired of feeling rushed. I wanted time for reflection, dialogue, and fun at the end of each day for both the students and me. Thus began the development of our daily closing meeting.

I knew that if I wanted students to reflect, I had to teach them how to be reflective. Our children are growing up constantly rushed from one activity to the next. They are in motion from the time they climb out of bed in the morning until the time they climb back into bed at night. They have no time to sit back, take a deep breath, and reflect.

I also knew that if reflection were to become an integral part of class life, not just a "tack-on," I needed to teach students how to be reflective throughout the day. I began building five minutes into each activity or lesson just for reflection. After we finished—or even when we were in the middle of—math activities, recess games, academic choice times, class meetings, or class projects, we'd stop and talk about what worked well, what didn't, what was fun, what wasn't, and why.

The end-of-the-day closing meeting became a natural outgrowth of this work together. I stopped the last academic class earlier than before: between 3:00 and 3:05. Next, to make for a calmer ending, we took care of the "business" type things—classroom jobs, packing up belongings to go home and such—before our closing meeting. Then at 3:15, with all that activity done, we met in a circle to close our day.

Reflecting on the Day

I often began by telling the children to take a couple of deep breaths and a few quiet moments so we could all be ready to participate fully in the meeting. After this quiet time, we would celebrate the hard work we had done that day in both the academic and social arenas. I would ask, "What went well as a class today?" or "What did we really work hard on today as a class?" I'd take just a couple of ideas. A child might say that he noticed how hard people were working on their autobiographies during writing time. Another child might say that she noticed people were remembering to raise their hands to speak instead of calling out.

Next, I'd ask what the class noticed that we might need to work on. Again, one or two children would share their ideas. This part of the meeting also told me about things I needed to reteach, model, and practice with the children, or possibly things that needed to go on our agenda for a problem-solving class meeting.

In the next part of the meeting, the children would focus on themselves as individuals. I usually offered a question or thought that would focus the children's thinking. Here are some examples:

* Rate your day on a scale of 1–10, and give one reason for your rating.

* What was your favorite part of the day?

* What was something helpful or friendly that you did today?

* Give one word to describe your learning today.

How to Play Aroostasha

Have students stand in a circle with their hands clasped in front of them (fingers interlaced).

1. Chant "Aroostasha, aroostasha, aroostasha-sha," while moving your clasped hands from the right side of your body to the left, and pulsing your hands up and down to the beat. Then do the chant while moving your hands back to the right side of your body, pulsing to the beat as you go. Have your class repeat the chant and body movements after you.

2. Call out "Thumbs up." Repeat step 1, with both hands clasped and thumbs up.

3. Call out "thumbs up, wrists together." Do step 1 again, with hands clasped, thumbs up, and wrists together.

4. Call out "thumbs up, wrists together, elbows in." Do step 1 with hands clasped, thumbs up, wrists together, and elbows in. By now your class should be able to do the movements as soon as you call out the instruction without first having to see you demonstrate.

Keep going in this manner, adding one body position at a time. For example, you can add knees together, toes in, bottom out, tongue out. (Ever try to say "Aroostasha" with your tongue out? Kids will really get a laugh out of this!)

* Give a gesture to describe your feelings today.

* Name one thing you were grateful for today.

* What was one new thing you learned today?

* What was one thing you were proud of today?

* What was one thing that was hard today?

After I gave the focus question and a minute or two of silent reflection time, one child would volunteer to start. We decided to use a Koosh ball as the talking piece. The child holding the Koosh ball could talk if he or she wanted to. That child would then give the ball to the next person in the circle. The ball would travel all the way around, giving anyone who wanted to talk an opportunity to do so without having to raise his or her hand.

Of course, because of time, we decided to limit each child to saying up to three sentences. (Giving a specific and focused question also helped limit how much each person said.) The children also had the option to pass when the Koosh ball came to them. Giving the ball to the next person without saying anything signified a pass.

After everyone who wanted to share (including me) had spoken, I would ask a few children to summarize, make connections, and share observations about the class's reflections.

Finally, our meeting would often close with something fun, like singing a couple of verses of a favorite song. I would then dismiss a few children at a time to pick up their book bags and coats from their desks, stack their chairs, and line up.

Variations on the Format

Depending on how the day had gone, I would vary the format of the closing meeting. Some days we'd feel exhausted and overwhelmed. We'd then decide as a class to skip the reflection and dialogue, going straight to doing something to energize ourselves and make us laugh together. Usually we'd get up and sing a silly song or do "Aroostasha" (see page 20), and we'd all leave feeling relaxed and exhilarated.

Other days, the children would be so interested in the current read-aloud book that we'd decide to finish it during our closing meeting.

Sometimes the class would have so much to say that we'd bring our journals to the carpet and spend part of our closing meeting doing some writing about our day before talking about it.

There are lots of ways to bring closure to a day of hard work. The important thing is to read your class and decide what will best meet everyone's needs on that particular afternoon.

After the closing meeting was up and running in our classroom, life at the end of the day looked dramatically different: twenty-eight children and me sitting calmly in a circle with all the day's business behind us, a Koosh ball being passed around the circle, children commenting reflectively about the day. The meeting comes to an end as the class sings "Dreamer," one of our favorites. The bell rings and the children and I exit feeling a sense of closure and peace, humming a few bars of "Dreamer."

Now that's what I call a good ending!

Power in Speech

Coaching Children to Assert Themselves through Respectful Talk

BY MEGAN EARLS

One of the most valuable things we can teach students is how to assert themselves in respectful ways. In spontaneous and planned moments throughout the day, teachers can help students think about what they want to communicate, examine their words, and try new and different ways of speaking.

But who has time to let children talk, we teachers often ask, when standardized tests are upon us starting from September and many of our students are reading below grade level? Perhaps we also fear behavior problems. For many years, I thought it would be easier to keep students quiet than to negotiate a conversation, especially in the upper grades.

But when I think back on my most valuable lessons in childhood—the moments I am most proud of—I see they are times when I spoke up. The ability to speak up assertively and respectfully is a form of power that helps our students succeed in school and in life. If I keep the classroom silent, I'm robbing students of this power.

Despite the concerns about falling behind or, worse, inviting chaos by encouraging talk, I have found that when children know how to talk skillfully, behavior problems decrease. I do less talking and more teaching. Students learn more each day, finding new strength in their academic and social lives as they find their voices.

Here are some strategies that I've found helpful in coaching talk among fifth graders in two kinds of situations: spontaneous teachable moments and planned discussions.

Teachable Moments

Students' school days are filled with moments of conflict or awk- wardness that can be positively handled with the skillful use of talk. Coaching students through these times involves:

❋ Being alert to such moments

❋ Giving students an opening to "do over" using more constructive talk

❋ Suggesting words to students when needed and demonstrating an appropriate tone of voice

EXAMPLE: THE STEPPED-ON COAT

It's the end of the day, and the class is packing their bags, talking about their after-school plans. But it's getting too loud. I see Terrence and Laquasia talking loudly, possibly angrily, at each other. I flick the lights, signaling the class to stop, look at me, and listen up.

"It's too loud in here. Pack-up time needs to be calmer so everyone can get organized." I walk over to Laquasia and Terrence, who are looking upset.

"What's happening here?" I ask.

I learn that Terrence just threw Laquasia's coat on the floor. He says she had stepped on his and that's why he threw hers down. Laquasia confirms the story, but neither of them knows what comes next.

"Terrence, what other way could you respond that's respectful but that gets your point across?"

Terrence pauses, then turns to Laquasia and says, "Oh, that's okay, Laquasia. Don't worry about it." He turns back to me, as if to say, "Is that okay?"

It is not okay, because although Terrance's response might sound respectful, it is not true to his feelings. I don't want students to think that being respectful means avoiding your own needs and feelings.

"I'm guessing, Terrence, that it's really not okay with you when someone steps on your coat," I say. "Watch me for a minute. Here's another way you could respond: 'Laquasia, I'm really mad right now. It's not okay for you to step all over my coat.'" In my demonstration, I make eye contact with Laquasia and use a strong voice without yelling. It's important to teach that our body language and tone of voice are just as important as the words we use.

Turning back to Terrence, I continue, "Terrence, now you can tell Laquasia what you would like her to do if this happens again. You could start with, 'Next time you see a coat on the floor, you could …'"

Terrence repeats the prompt and finishes with two excellent suggestions: hang it back up, or bring it to him at his desk.

Planned Discussions

Children do not come to school necessarily knowing how to engage in discussions about books, ideas, or social issues. They need to be actively taught discussion skills, just as they need to be actively taught how to read, write, do math, draw, or conduct a science experiment. Some helpful strategies in this teaching include:

* Agreeing with the class on some respectful and constructive phrases to use in different discussion situations

* Modeling and reminding students to use such phrases in class discussions

* Being alert to opportunities to show students not only how to agree or disagree with each other, but how to build on each other's ideas

EXAMPLE: A BOOK DISCUSSION

It's the middle of the year, and the class is partway through our read-aloud of *Sidewalk Story* by Sharon Bell Mathus. Early in the year, we had brainstormed some constructive phrases to use in holding a book discussion. Ideas included:

* "What do you think of …" (to ask a question)

* "I think …" (to share an idea we're working on)

* "I agree, and I'd like to add …" (to add onto an idea with more evidence or further thoughts)

24

- "What do you mean?" "Can you say more about that?" or "So, is what you're saying …?" (when we can't follow what someone is saying)

- "I don't see it that way. What about …?" (when we disagree with someone's idea)

We had written these phrases on a big chart and had been practicing using them. On this day, the students are sharing their thoughts about Lilly, the main character in *Sidewalk Story*, and her best friend Tanya.

I want the class to see that we can use talk not only to question each other's ideas, but to build on them.

"Usually in starting a conversation about a book, it helps to begin with an idea you're working on or a question," I remind the class. "Who can get us started?"

Five or six hands go up. Nica offers her idea. "I think Lilly's mom is really mean. She's always yelling at Lilly."

The students think about this for a moment and then begin to talk. "I agree, and Lilly doesn't even deserve to be yelled at," Michael says.

"That's true, but I don't think the mom's really mean. She's more like, worried," Marcos responds.

So far so good. The students are listening to each other, agreeing and disagreeing respectfully, moving the discussion along.

Then, Malek makes a comment and an excited Nica responds by saying, "No, but Lilly's mom isn't …"

I catch Nica's eye and gesture toward our chart of respectful discussion phrases the class agreed on. Nica starts again. "I don't see it that way, Malek. What about …?" The students pick up on the correction, but the interruption to the discussion is minimal and they continue easily.

Later in the conversation, Jeremy makes a comment that is too far from the story. "Tanya's mom and Lilly's mom probably had a fight or something, so that's why they hate each other."

25

There is no evidence of such a fight in the book. Seeing this as a chance to model how to handle such a situation in a discussion, I say, "I agree it could happen that the two mothers would have a fight. But I don't remember anything in the book that says they did. Do you?"

"No, I guess not," Jeremy says.

At this point I want the class to see that we can use talk not only to question each other's ideas, but to build on them. So I say, "But you're getting at something here, Jeremy. The mothers don't fight, but they don't help each other out. Do you have an idea about that?"

Jeremy thinks a minute, then begins to talk about how Lilly's mom might not be helping because she doesn't want to get her own family in trouble.

I look around the circle and remind the class, "Now would be a smart time to go inside the book and see if we can get some backup for Jeremy's idea." We are quiet for a minute as we think about which scenes in the book might have what we're looking for. Jeremy sits tall, knowing the class is invested in his thinking, but also understanding that his ideas are more powerful when he expresses them accurately and without exaggeration. The class, meanwhile, has learned a way to disagree respectfully and move a discussion constructively toward more sound ideas.

Hard but Necessary Work

Teaching students how to talk can be hard work. When our daily schedules are accounted for down to the minute, it's hard to slow down to have these conversations. It might seem easier not to teach talk. But it's scary to think what children would miss. We need to prepare them to be respectful and assertive in their lives, and there are bigger problems they'll face than a couple of winter coats thrown on the floor or a sloppily constructed idea about a book. But those are good places to start. From those modest beginnings, children can learn to speak up in the world—inside and outside our classrooms.

Including Wyatt

How *Responsive Classroom* Strategies Supported a Child with Special Needs

BY NANCY KOVACIC

Morning Meeting is about to start. With eye contact and a head nod, Wyatt chooses a friend to ring the chime that signals our gathering. We come together in record time. There is a feeling of anticipation as we silently watch Wyatt get his wheelchair positioned so that he can take his turn leading Morning Meeting.

Wyatt is a bright, cheerful third grader. He has a powerful will and a tremendous appetite for sharing learning and laughter with his classmates. He also has cerebral palsy, which has left him with very limited control of his muscles of movement and speech. When I learned that Wyatt would be in my class, I wondered and worried about finding ways to include him. Would the other children help him join their work groups? Would he be able to work and play as one of us?

I soon found my worries dissipating. Wyatt's friends in Room 34 were taught to communicate with him by asking yes/no questions. They waited patiently for him to dip his chin for "yes" or turn his head to one side for "no." Our classroom climate and practices reinforced the expectation that Wyatt would be a respected

Nancy Kovacic

member of the group, and the children willingly made the small adjustments that enabled him to participate fully in classroom life.

Many things made Wyatt's third grade year a successful one. His teachers and therapists found technologies to help him communicate and coached him in his social skills. His parents involved themselves in classroom life. Many of the students in Room 34 had known Wyatt since kindergarten and loved him for the endearing person that he is.

And the *Responsive Classroom* approach, with its emphasis on empathy, respect, and community, was another key element.

When Wyatt joined our class, I had been using the approach for ten years. During that year, I saw how *Responsive Classroom* teaching strategies supported all the other critical efforts aimed at helping Wyatt be a full member of the class. Morning Meeting, Academic Choice, and Rules and Logical Consequences were particularly useful.

Morning Meeting

From our first day of school together, Morning Meeting helped establish a climate in which every student could feel a sense of belonging and significance. This daily half-hour routine helped us function as a unit—working, playing, and learning together. Each meeting begins with Greeting, in which every child receives a friendly, respectful salute. Next comes Sharing, designed to help every child know and be known by classmates. Over the course of every two weeks or so, all students get a turn at sharing some news, and sharers practice calling on different classmates for questions and comments. In Group Activity, the emphasis is again on cooperation so that everyone can participate. Finally, in Morning Message, an important purpose is building community through shared written information.

With a warm smile, eye contact, and a voice "borrowed" from his DynaVox (a machine that played recorded phrases aloud when Wyatt pressed a control with his headpiece), Wyatt participated in all parts of our Morning Meeting. For example, silently passing the Koosh ball around the circle was a favorite class greeting. Holding the ball in his hand, Wyatt locked a "greeting gaze" onto one of his classmates. The greeted child then took the ball from Wyatt, returned his gaze and smile, and passed the ball to another child.

For Sharing, our Monday-morning "Weekend Whip Share" was a favorite. We zipped twice around the circle, each child giving two or three intriguing words about her or his weekend. To help Wyatt participate, his mother recorded weekend news on his DynaVox or sent a note with a few details about something he did, such as going to a baseball game or museum. On days when we did individual interactive sharings and it was Wyatt's turn, Sharon Magera, his adult assistant, would have a yes/no conversation with him while the class listened. Wyatt then made eye contact with a classmate whose question he was ready to answer. His wide smile showed the pure pleasure of sharing his weekend with his friends.

A favorite Group Activity was the Shoe Game, in which everyone takes off one shoe, places it in the middle of the floor, and hides the shoed foot. Each person takes a turn choosing a shoe from the pile, guessing the owner, and returning the shoe with a friendly comment, such as "I think I found your shoe, Kathy." Sharon helped Wyatt join this activity by placing his shoe in the circle. When his turn came, Wyatt used his eye lock to show his guess as to the shoe's owner.

As for Morning Message, I would usually include a survey question on the chart. For example, I might write "Which story do you want to publish?" and give, as choices, stories the class had been working on. First thing in the morning, before the meeting, the children would show their choice with a tally mark. To help Wyatt participate, one student would ask him yes/no questions and make his mark for him. As we read the choices aloud during the meeting, the children would stomp softly to show their choice. With Sharon's help, Wyatt would show his choice by pounding lightly on the tray of his wheelchair.

Morning Meeting gave the children a chance to connect with their classmates and ease into the day ahead. This was especially important for Wyatt because he would be in many other places during the day, including physical and speech therapy sessions. His engaged presence in the morning helped establish him as a member of our group, even if he was often physically absent.

> Wyatt's engaged presence in the morning helped establish him as a member of our group, even if he was often physically absent.

> The climate of acceptance and cooperation that we established together helped each child feel acknowledged, appreciated, and heard.

Academic Choice

When teachers use Academic Choice to structure a lesson, they give students options for what to learn or how to go about their learning to reach the goal of the lesson. Students can then choose options that are appropriately challenging and interesting to them. Having this kind of choice was helpful to Wyatt. For example, physically acting out a poem or a scene from a story in a reading group was impossible for him, but nonphysical options were always available. And because all of the children were given choices, Wyatt didn't feel singled out.

For one of our research projects, all students chose an animal they wanted to learn about. Wyatt chose the king snake. With help from his speech therapist and his work partner, Jack, Wyatt designed the cards for the slide presentation on his chosen creature.

Rules and Logical Consequences

The *Responsive Classroom* approach to discipline stresses including all children in rule creation and applying logical consequences consistently for any student who does not live by the rules. All children are responsible for making the classroom a safe and friendly place. This was yet another element that helped establish Wyatt as a full member of the community.

As Wyatt began third grade, he was ready to make a big leap in taking responsibility for the way his behavior affected the learning community. Understandably, Wyatt experienced much frustration because of his limited means of expressing his thoughts and feelings. Sometimes when he became frustrated, he would cry instead of communicating with his DynaVox. But the group of adults working with Wyatt believed that he was capable of learning greater self-control and that it was important to hold him to the same standard of behavior required of his classmates. Therefore, if Wyatt could not or would not quiet himself, Sharon helped him by using a modified version of our class time-out procedure.

Once separated from the situation in which self-control had become difficult, Wyatt would take a few minutes to sit by himself and regain composure. Before returning to the group, he would take the extra step of using his DynaVox to show his intention for handling himself should such a situation arise again. Wyatt's choices included "straight breathing," one of the calming strategies he'd learned from Dr. Rap, our school psychologist. Another choice was to call up his "inner voice," a set of calming words that Wyatt would think to himself. The words, which special education teacher Donna Nordone (a *Responsive Classroom* consulting teacher for our district) and speech therapist Gladys Millman helped him practice all year, were "As a class member, I have to do my part. When I'm in the classroom, I have to use a calm and quiet voice so others can learn and work. This helps me and my friends."

Wyatt's participation in time-out was an important way to show all the children that the rules applied to everyone in the class. Plus, the other children could see that, just like them, Wyatt needed help with gaining self-control. And Wyatt learned empathy as he began to see how his behavior could be disruptive or helpful to his classmates' learning. As with all other aspects of our classroom life, when it came to discipline, Wyatt was like everyone else.

Including Everyone Helps Everyone Learn

The *Responsive Classroom* approach helped Room 34 be a place where every child had an equal chance to learn and grow. The climate of acceptance and cooperation that we established together helped each child feel acknowledged, appreciated, and heard. That enabled the class members, including Wyatt, to help each other take risks with their social and academic learning. As a result, our year with Wyatt was a year of growth for all of us.

Editor's note: To learn more about the *Responsive Classroom* strategies discussed in this article, see the following books from Northeast Foundation for Children:

* *The Morning Meeting Book* by Roxann Kriete

* *Learning Through Academic Choice* by Paula Denton, EdD

* *Rules in School* by Kathryn Brady, Mary Beth Forton, Deborah Porter, and Chip Wood

Teaching FOR Active Learning

The Teacher Is the Textbook

BY CHIP WOOD

"Teacher empowerment" is a term loosely thrown around these days in journals, conferences, and in-service workshops. But what is it that we want to be empowered to do?

Most teachers of young children believe that there is something drastically wrong with kindergarten and primary grade expectations. And we would like to do something about it.

"But," we ask, "what can I do? I'm only one teacher. How can I make a difference?"

Many of us say the same things:

* "You know, I can hardly bear to give that test at the end of kindergarten. For the first time I see kids' lights go out. They think, 'I failed; I'm no good.'"

* "All year long I tell the kids, 'You can do it!' Then I have to test them and show them they can't."

* "I'm forever telling kids to hurry up. There's so much to cover. I know I'll never get it all done. If I feel that way, how must the kids feel?"

35

* "The first grade teachers tell us our kids better be ready; the second grade teachers tell the first grade teachers to get them ready."

* "There's so much to get through. I can't stand it!"

* "I've never seen such stressed-out kids."

* "Kindergarten isn't much of a garden anymore."

How would we like it to be different?

Many of us would argue for a return to a more playful school beginning. We should advocate strongly for this position to protect the welfare of the children we teach. Spontaneous play is the foundation of imagination, insight, and ethical behavior in children. These qualities are not fully developed in children prior to the age of five! Kindergarten is not the time for children to stop playing, to start behaving like miniature adults in their school offices. In kindergarten and first grade play takes on significant new meaning. Instructive play allows children experience and experimentation with critical thinking and judgment, problem-solving, decision-making. When children are denied these possibilities in an active learning environment, they suffer from what Marie Winn describes as "play deprivation." (Winn 1983, 80-83)

Such deprivation stunts the mental and emotional growth of our young. By focusing so singularly on academic achievement at an early age, we are truly shortchanging our children. The very skills high school teachers tell us their students lack—independent study skills, initiative, perseverance, creativity, critical thinking—all have their beginnings in play. Without the foundation of play, these essential human qualities may not be replaceable. We can certainly train generations of technicians without allowing play, but we will educate few explorers, teach few inventors. Dorothy Cohen warned us in 1972 that "children are being slowly compressed into a largely passive existence. They sit at school, sit through television, sit through after-school homework, lessons in music, art, crafts, religion and foreign language. When they play, it is all too often under adult supervision and according to adult rules." (Cohen 1972, 337)

In order to guarantee play its proper place in our classrooms, to restore it to the curriculum, we must also stand for some limitations on pencil and paper academics. Not only are curricula expectations often inappropriate, but the sheer volume of required paperwork for the children and for us allows no time for essential observation, teacher-child interaction, humanness.

Here are three down-to-earth, practical principles that we can agree on and achieve. Let us make the following statements to our school boards, our administrators, our parents, and the publishers.

1. No more formalized textbook-workbook reading program instruction prior to first grade.

2. No more workbook math prior to first grade.

3. No more standardized achievement testing prior to third grade.

Why are these three admonitions so important and what positive practices should we forward in their stead?

1. As teachers we are being denied the opportunity to teach reading readiness the way that we know is most beneficial to children and the most fun. We can do without a textbook program because we can do a better job! Through immersion in a language-rich environment of poetry, songs, rhymes, labeling, drawing and writing, children begin reading. We can teach children to love literature, instill in them a desire to be lifelong readers, not just premature decoders. It is the teacher who must teach reading readiness, not the textbook.

2. Math can be intriguing, practical, and playful. We limit the scope of children's mathematical abilities by plunking them down in computational workbooks before they have learned to love the manipulation of quantities. Calculators and computers will increasingly compute for us. Our job is to give children a love for scientific and mathematical inquiry, and to help them understand that they can control the ideas of math as well as the operations. Teachers need to spend more time creating opportunities for mathematical exploration, less time correcting workbook and ditto pages.

3. Measurement and evaluation of student growth and performance is essential for our accountability and important to parents. Testing, prior to third grade, is simply not the best way to achieve this goal. Teachers know more than the tests can tell, and young children are damaged by overexposure to testing environments. Providing teachers time to teach, observe, record behavior, and measure children according to normative expectations in cognitive development and in social, emotional, and adaptive growth is a far better use of professional teachers than requiring them to spend time administering and scoring academic measures. Teachers also need more time for communicating

directly with parents and more time for holding parent conferences to review behavior and share expectations.

How might we stem the tide? How might we work together to accomplish three simple goals that would help restore our primacy as teachers in the classroom? How can we make early elementary grades a place for children again?

In each community we must work together to advocate for change. We must advocate through education. We must organize! As groups of teachers we can:

* Present our ideas and theories to the school board and administrative councils, helping them to understand the needs of young children.

* Ask these people to visit our classrooms.

* Hold parent meetings on child development and simultaneously invite parents to observe and participate in our rooms. Parents are our best allies.

* Help parents to make good preschool choices.

* Work with nursery schools and day cares to explain our expectations in the elementary school.

* Take the lead in exposing the dangers of too much paper/pencil too soon.

* Ask for time for professional development, in-service training, cooperative planning time.

In order to be empowered to teach the way we know is best for children, we must organize and work together for change. Early childhood committees and task forces are being formed in community after community. This is our chance to make a difference. There are allies in every parent and administrators group. Join with them to return the classroom to the children and teaching to the teacher.

Works Cited

Cohen, Dorothy. 1972. *The Learning Child*. New York: Pantheon Books.

Winn, Marie. 1983. *Children Without Childhood*. New York: Penguin Books.

Active Games for Active Bodies

Ideas for Bringing Physical Activity into the Classroom

BY MARK FARNSWORTH

C hildren need plenty of opportunities throughout the school day to be active. Their bodies need to move—not just once a week in gym class but throughout the day, especially during the winter months when there are fewer opportunities to play outdoors.

This is a time when teachers see the effects of pent-up energy: Children seem fidgety and restless and have a hard time maintaining focus. Providing children with frequent opportunities to use their physical energy is a proactive strategy which can help prevent these problems while at the same time increasing children's ability to concentrate on their learning. One easy way to provide these opportunities is to incorporate simple active games into your daily routine.

Many teachers using the *Responsive Classroom* approach already use active games during Morning Meeting. Here I suggest three other times when you might want to use active games in your classroom. The types of games I'm suggesting can be

> When tension is high, rather than moving right into the next academic activity, take a few minutes to play an active game.

played in ten minutes or less, yet will go a long way toward keeping energy high and concentration strong in the classroom (not to mention strengthening children's sense of belonging and inclusion).

When Children Need to Wait

The bus driver for a field trip is ten minutes late; children are at the rug waiting for Morning Meeting to begin; students have formed a line to go to lunch, but the lunchroom monitor has not yet arrived. These are times when children can frequently use pent-up energy in nonproductive ways—nudging each other in line, wrestling while waiting at the meeting circle, etc. A structured game for children to play at these times can provide a positive outlet for their energy and also make transitions smoother. Here is one of many possible games you can teach your students to play when there is waiting time.

GAME SUGGESTION: "DUM DUM DA DA"

This quick rhythmic game can be easily varied to suit your needs.

The teacher begins by chanting *dum dum da da*, making a movement for each syllable. For example, I might begin:

> dum (clap hands)
> dum (clap hands)
> da (pat knee)
> da (pat knee)

The students then repeat the chant with the accompanying movement. I often begin very slowly, then speed it up, then gradually bring it back to a slow pace. You can also try going from small motor movements such as snapping fingers to whole body movements such as touching toes and jumping high in the sky. Or you can go from silent to loud and back to silent again. I often end this game with gentle silent motions such as tapping your shoulders or nodding your head as a way of signaling that the game is over and it's time to move on to the next activity.

When Tension Is High

You've just finished a serious conversation concerning water pollution; your class has spent the morning taking the state achievement tests; there's been a long class meeting about a problem in the classroom. The air feels heavy and you sense the need for some lightening before moving on to the next activity.

Tension can greatly limit children's ability to concentrate. At times like these when it is high, rather than moving right into the next academic activity, take a few minutes to play an active game. The chance to relax, laugh, and have fun together will help to reduce tension and improve concentration.

GAME SUGGESTION:
"HOW DO YOU LIKE YOUR NEIGHBORS?"

Players sit in a circle. There are enough chairs or designated places for everyone to sit in the circle except the leader. The leader is in the center. Everyone is given a number. The leader asks a player, "How do you like your neighbors?" The player can offer one of two replies. If the player says, "Very well," then all the players jump to their feet and change seats. If the player says, "I'd like new neighbors," the leader then asks, "Who would you like for new neighbors?" The player answers with two numbers (for example, "5 and 12"). The players with these numbers then change places with the players seated to the left and right of the player who called the numbers. Each time players change seats, the leader also tries to sit in one of the vacant seats. The person left standing becomes the new leader.

When Energy Is Low

It's mid-afternoon, students have been sitting for several hours, eyelids are heavy, bodies are drooping. Now is the time for a game that requires children to stretch and move their bodies. Afterwards, they'll be more energetic and much more able to focus on the work at hand. Here's a good energizing game, especially useful for those after-lunch-time blues.

41

This game can be used as an energizer or transition activity. It begins with the teacher saying: "I see!" The class responds, "What do you see?" The teacher responds, "I see bubbles floating in the air." The students act out that idea until the teacher says, "I see." All the students stop again and respond: "What do you see?" The game continues with the teacher (or student leader) suggesting another idea.

Here are some suggestions to get started. Of course you will choose movements that suit your students. Older children will probably not want to be "bees buzzing around," but they may enjoy pretending to be rock-and-roll stars or star athletes. Try calling out movements that move from the very slow to the very active and back to the slow again to end the game. By ending with a command similar to "I see students walking quietly to their chairs," you can easily end the game and help children move into the next activity.

"I see children hopping all around."

"I see planes flying through the sky."

"I see puppy dogs sleeping on the ground."

"I see cowboys riding horses."

"I see bees buzzing around."

"I see rockets zooming to the moon."

"I see my friends walking to our line spot."

"I see my friends quietly putting away their materials."

Teaching the Games

When you play an active game in the classroom, you want it to be lively and fun, but you also want it to feel safe and comfortable for every child in the group. Below are some guidelines to use when teaching children how to play an active game.

* *Clearly explain the rules and procedures. Follow with a demonstration.* Have a few children demonstrate what the game will look like: "What does it look like to jump safely?" "What does a gentle but firm hand clap look like?"

* *Be clear about your expectations for behavior.* The more specific you can be, the better. For example, if I were introducing the game "How do you like your neighbors?" I would use questions like the following to make sure that rules

and behavior expectations are clear: "How can we take care of each other?" "How can we move across the circle to change seats?" "What could you do if someone gets to a seat right before you do?" "What could you do to be a good sport if you're the last one standing?"

* *Monitor the game for success. Stop the game when it's not successful.* If the game's not working, stop it right away and figure out what went wrong. Perhaps the space needs to be made smaller or larger. Perhaps the game is too hard or too easy. Perhaps rules need to be clarified or practiced.

* *Find a way to join in the playing while still maintaining control.* Children love to have their teachers play with them, and many teachers enjoy the chance to play with their students. Find a way to play that allows real participation without losing your ability to monitor the pace and success of the game. Perhaps start outside the game and move into the game once you see it is working smoothly, or choose to play alongside a child who needs some extra support.

* *Change the pace of the game if necessary.* Keep an eye on whether the pace of the game seems right and be ready to speed it up or slow it down at any time in response to the needs of your group. Some games are only fun if they're played at a fast pace. In this case, the teacher would make sure that the game keeps moving quickly.

* *Don't overplay a game.* When games are overplayed, they become stale and children lose interest. Be aware of how children are responding to a particular game. Some games can be played over and over again without children losing enthusiasm; other games are best played once. Develop a repertoire of games and keep a running list in your classroom.

Editor's note: For more activity ideas, see *99 Activities and Greetings* by Melissa Correa-Connolly, published by Northeast Foundation for Children.

Knowledge Of Children
Yardsticks for Teachers

BY NEFC STAFF

Knowledge of developmental patterns is a powerful tool for teachers. It helps teachers make informed decisions about what to teach and how to teach, and it helps them to understand what children are going through at different ages.

For years, NEFC co-founder and consulting teacher Chip Wood has spoken with great clarity, humor, and warmth about the developmental characteristics of children at different ages. Three years ago, he consolidated his wealth of information into the concise, user-friendly resource for parents and teachers, *Yardsticks: Children in the Classroom Ages 4–12*. This year, *Yardsticks* was expanded to include ages 13 and 14 and was published by NEFC this month.

This article features excerpts from *Yardsticks* followed by several teachers' observations and classroom practices that respond to the developmental needs of children.

Six-Year-Olds

Rapid physical growth is mirrored in rapid physical activity … Along with great bursts of energy go periods of fatigue and frequent illnesses. The importance of friends now rivals the importance of parents and teachers in the child's social development. Classrooms full of six-year-olds are busy, noisy places. Talking, humming, whistling, bustling are the order of the day.

—**from *Yardsticks***

"Lively," "spontaneous," "social," "energetic," and "busy" are all words that come quickly to mind when Cynthia Donnelly thinks about six-year-olds. A first grade teacher at Kensington Avenue School in Springfield, Massachusetts, Cynthia has taught six-year-olds for nine years.

HANDS-ON

"You have to be flexible with sixes," says Cynthia. "Sometimes they're full of energy and bursting with enthusiasm. Other days they wear themselves out."

"Children at six like to be up and moving," notes Cynthia. "They need to have their hands on the materials and be actively involved when learning." Cynthia designs her lessons to include many hands-on activities.

She also has a choice time every morning. Some favorite choices are clay, puzzles, art projects, the listening center, and finger plays. Cynthia notes that this is a very industrious and social time of the day. "They love it and they need it," she says. Sometimes, in the middle of a choice period, her class will burst spontaneously into song. "Now that's what six is all about."

Cynthia's students love to work with classmates and to be physically close to one another. At writing time, children work at tables of four and six. "They especially like the six table," Cynthia points out, "and what they like even better, when I let them, is to cram nine chairs around this table so that they're sitting elbow to elbow."

BOOK BUDDIES

Having "book buddies" at reading time is another practice that allows her students to be close to one another. Book buddies begin a period of sustained silent reading sitting back to back. After ten minutes, they turn around to face one another and share their books. Sometimes they read a favorite passage to their buddy; sometimes they describe an exciting part.

Cynthia explains that at times it can be quite challenging to keep the bubbling energy and enthusiasm of the sixes focused, especially with twenty-six in one classroom. Sometimes the energy just bubbles right over, becoming unproductive.

> The eagerness, curiosity, imagination, drive, and enthusiasm of the six-year-old is perhaps never again matched in quantity or intensity during the life span.

"Having a case of the heebie-jeebies is what we call it when this happens in our room," explains Cynthia. "And sometimes we need to just stop whatever we're doing to get the heebie-jeebies out."

Singing and dancing work well. The children come to the circle, Cynthia puts on a Greg and Steve record, and the heebie-jeebies are released to the lively tune of "Body Rock." "It's just perfect for this," Cynthia says. "When we're done, the kids feel good and they're ready to focus again."

Cynthia sums up her thoughts about six-year-olds with a quote from *Yardsticks*. "There is a sentence in *Yardsticks* about sixes which I love," she says. "It states, 'The eagerness, curiosity, imagination, drive, and enthusiasm of the six-year-old is perhaps never again matched in quantity or intensity during the life span.' I couldn't agree more."

Nine-Year-Olds

The enthusiasm of eight often turns into dark brooding and worrying at nine—worrying about world events, about the health of parents, about moving away, about losing best friends, about changing schools … Nines complain about their aches and pains, their cuts and bruises and their hurt feelings … Teachers of nine-year-olds in third and fourth grade need a sense of humor and a determined lightness to challenge the sometimes deadly seriousness of the age. Their growing peer solidarity can be channeled into wonderful club activities—e.g., stamps, chess, rocks. Positive language is also essential for children's growth. An ounce of negative criticism is greatly magnified by the nine-year-old. An ounce of encouragement is as well.

—from *Yardsticks*

Timmy Sheyda, a fourth grade teacher at Greenfield Center School in Massachusetts, uses a variety of strategies to keep levity and perspective in his fourth grade classroom. As nine is often an age when children are hard on themselves and each other, nines need teachers who can balance this tendency and keep a positive tone in the classroom.

GROUP BUILDING

Timmy often begins the year with activities such as trust exercises and group challenges to build community spirit. This year, his class took a trip to a nearby nature center to do a

ropes course and other group initiative exercises. Timmy observes that his fourth graders "are ready to grapple with some fairly complex social and ethical issues" as they are beginning to understand the complexities of what it takes to get along with one another.

These group-building exercises help his students make many discoveries in a short period of time. They quickly recognize the importance of communicating effectively, listening to others, and giving encouragement as they attempt these group challenges. These are skills that they will continue to build and refine in the classroom as they work through the many social issues that arise throughout the year.

A PLAYFUL SPIRIT

While his students struggle with the challenges of this age, Timmy works to keep a playful and positive spirit intact in his classroom. On the walls, there are visual reminders that speak in a fanciful way to the sometimes critical tendencies of the nine-year-old: "We Brook No Self-Deprecation Here" reads one handwritten sign. Timmy's students know that he loves to play with language and use what they call "juicy words."

This language play shows up throughout the day as Timmy frequently uses puns, jokes, and riddles in his conversation with students. He also uses language play on the Morning Message chart. His students often find secret messages to decode, riddles to solve, or vocabulary words to unscramble as their first challenge in the morning.

Having a good sense of humor helps when teaching fourth grade, says Timmy. "We're dealing with a lot of serious issues," he explains. "It's important to be able to inject humor at opportune moments to relieve the tension."

Sometimes in the middle of a tense discussion, he'll begin to doodle on the board. His students will look up to find fanciful caricatures and creatures that can't help but make them laugh. "It gives us a breather," says Timmy. "I want my students to feel like they've done some hard work by the end of the fourth grade, but I also want them to have had fun."

Thirteen-Year-Olds

For most thirteen-year-olds, school is a series of classrooms, a series of teachers, a rotating series of groups of peers ... While many middle and junior high schools are now moving to block scheduling and teaming, providing settings where students actually get more social interaction, these schools remain in the minority ... Cognitive growth is enhanced in those environments that foster and respect social interaction.

—from Yardsticks

The need to know and be known by classmates, to have a forum to share news and a playful time together—under the guidance of a caring adult—is as great at thirteen as at many earlier ages. Maybe greater.

One way that some seventh and eighth grade teachers are addressing this need is by using a middle school version of Morning Meeting to fit the developmental needs of their students and the schedule of their school day.

CIRCLE OF POWER AND RESPECT

In eighth grade classrooms at Stuart Hobson Middle School in Washington, DC, students begin their day with Circle of Power and Respect (CPR). During CPR, students and teacher greet each other, listen to each other's news, feelings and ideas, and talk about the business of the school day ahead.

"It's a far more personal way to begin the day, sitting in a circle facing each other, making eye contact, than the old fashioned homeroom period, where students sat in rows looking at the backs of heads, hearing announcements from a faceless voice over the PA system," commented one teacher.

Often schools make time for this to happen by adapting, sometimes extending a bit, the first period of the day that was previously called "homeroom." Skeptics sometimes worry that this will take away from valuable academic time; teachers who do it, however, report that students' increased motivation to get to school on time, their improved attendance, and the overall improvement in attitude and motivation far outweigh the few minutes given to structure CPR into the day.

GREETINGS

Circle of Power and Respect begins with a structured greeting activity. Sometimes it is a simple "Good Morning, Ella—Good Morning, Natasha" passed around the circle. Sometimes it is more elaborate.

At Community Prep School in Providence, Rhode Island, eighth graders in Todd Zeigler's classroom greet each other in the manner of a chosen adjective: "This morning we will greet each other in a haughty way," announces their teacher. As well as being a vocabulary builder, this lends a playful touch and allows students to name and try out different mannerisms. Some other adjectives they've used include "dignified," "exuberant," and "charming."

Another favorite greeting at Community Prep is "Roll Call," a chant from Baltimore *Responsive Classroom* teacher Barbara McCutcheon. This greeting invites students to play with the notion of identities.

> *(unison)* Roll Call, Check the Beat
> Check, Check, Check the Beat
> Roll Call, Check the Beat
> Check, Check, Check the Beat
>
> *(first student, while the rest of class still clapping the beat)* My name is Matthew,
> They call me Matt
> I'm a soccer player, That's what I am.
>
> *(unison)* That's what he is, That's what
> he is. Roll Call, Check the Beat …

Some days at CPR, there might be a guest speaker talking about her career or talking about neighborhood volunteer opportunities. Other days, there is time for students to help each other with homework or a test-taking tips clinic, a current events discussion or a word game. Common to all the activities during CPR is the building of the vital skills of communication and cooperation within a supportive atmosphere.

That kind of genuine support is built upon understanding, which in turn is built upon knowledge of another person. CPR provides a time and a way for students to gain that knowledge of all class members—not just those they already term "friends."

They come to know whose grandmother is sick, whose brother is in a play, whose parent just got a new job. They know who loves to play soccer and who struggles with math. Even an apparently simple greeting like Roll Call can reveal so much—how we look at ourselves, what we are proud of, what nicknames we want to be called.

Sandra Jenkins, an eighth grade teacher at Stuart Hobson Middle School, asked her students what CPR meant to them. This is what one child wrote:

"There were so many students in my class that I hardly ever talked to and knew nothing about. But with CPR that has definitely changed. I can now sit down and have a good conversation with almost anyone. I've learned that so many people share the same interests as I. I've also learned that everyone deserves an equal amount of respect. There is no one person better than another. It's amazing what sitting in a circle and talking openly can do. CPR has opened up a whole new world for me."

Support for Teachers

Chip Wood's *Yardsticks* supports teachers in creating appropriate environments and curricula for their students. These "yardsticks" are intended to help teachers and parents understand what children are going through without limiting the children or burdening them with unrealistic expectations.

The book also reminds readers that each child's development will reflect his or her individuality even though it fits within a broad developmental pattern. "Although the patterns are universal," says Chip, "each child is unique—each child a gift, each child a surprise."

What Do Insects Do All Day?

How Academic Choice Can Spark Children's Desire to Learn

BY MARGARET BERRY WILSON

Four classes of second graders have just begun a new science unit on insects at the University School of Nashville in Tennessee. I and the other three second grade teachers have each invited our classes to share what they know about insects and what they would like to learn. To our delight, the children are bubbling over with comments and questions.

They excitedly share their knowledge: "Flies have big, bulging eyes," someone declares. "When a bee stings, it dies," says another student.

The children share their questions, too. "How many bees live in a hive?" asks one child. "What do insects *do* all day?" wonders another. Starting new units by helping children explore their knowledge and interests is a technique many teachers use. For the insect unit, we decided to do this by using an Academic Choice activity. A *Responsive Classroom* strategy, Academic Choice is a way of structuring lessons to give children choices in how they'll meet defined learning goals.

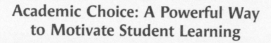

Academic Choice: A Powerful Way to Motivate Student Learning

A key *Responsive Classroom* strategy, Academic Choice is a way to structure lessons and activities. Teachers decide on the goal of the lesson or activity. They then give students options for what to learn or how to go about their learning to reach the defined goal.

Research has generally found that children have fewer behavior problems when they have regular opportunities to make choices in their learning.

Many teachers give children choices of how or what to learn. But what sets Academic Choice apart—and what is essential to its success—is its three-phase process of planning, working, and reflecting.

Planning. After the teacher introduces the activity choices, students plan what they're going to do and sometimes how they'll do it. For example, to show their knowledge about where bats live, first graders might choose whether to draw, build with blocks, or make a cut-and-paste picture. They might also decide whether to work with partners or alone.

Working. During this phase, children complete their chosen task. The teacher offers guidance as necessary.

Reflecting. After completing the chosen task, the children reflect on their work and their learning. They may think and write privately or present their work to the class. Reflection helps children make sense of their concrete experiences.

For more information, see *Learning Through Academic Choice* by Paula Denton, EdD, published by Northeast Foundation for Children.

Having choices gives children a way to connect learning to their personal interests and learning styles. Using Academic Choice to structure our introductory insect lesson really paid off for our second graders. This is how it worked.

Careful Lesson Planning

As a team, we planned the lesson with the straightforward learning goal of having children accurately reflect about and demonstrate what they already knew about insects. We had a secondary goal of inspiring enthusiasm and curiosity, but we decided to share only the first goal with the students.

In deciding what choices the children would have for demonstrating their insect knowledge, we brainstormed about materials that our classes had previously enjoyed and used successfully. How could they use those materials to show information about insects? We decided to give them the choices of writing, drawing with colored pencils, using pattern blocks, doing cut-and-paste pictures, or using modeling clay.

We wanted the students to be ready to share verbally what they knew about insects on that introductory day, while their minds were still busy with the topic. Most of their work, therefore, would occur in one long session—about forty-five minutes. We would give the children a relatively short planning option: They would simply think for a few minutes about which medium they would like to use to show their knowledge and then sign up on a choice board.

As for the reflection phase of this lesson, we wanted the whole class, not just a few students, to share their insect knowledge. To allow that to happen, we decided to invite all the children to present their work during periods spread throughout the day. As the children shared their morning's work, they would choose one or two facts to add to our class list of what we knew about insects. Then, the next day, we would brainstorm what we still wanted to find out.

Teaching the Lesson

As we put our plans into action, all four of us were happy to see that Academic Choice was indeed helping the children learn. They worked hard, asked insightful questions, and were clearly excited about beginning the new science unit.

In my classroom, students very quickly got to work after choosing their medium. As the students worked, they shared ideas with friends. A busy hum arose in the room. Many children were impressed with unusual facts their classmates casually shared. For instance, Maggie, who chose to write about flies, told friends that flies turn their food into "goo" and then slurp it. Alden delighted in his clay models of a wasp hanging out in a tree and a smaller insect on the ground. He used the models to show other children how certain wasps paralyze their prey and then eat the creatures while they're down.

In addition to sharing their knowledge as they worked, the children also questioned each other's facts and sometimes their own. Joshua used pattern blocks to show what he knew about dragonflies—he built the nymph as having six legs and the adult as having four. But as he did so, he began to doubt whether the four-legs fact was true. This self-questioning is a step toward rich learning.

The children became so involved in their projects that most needed the whole forty-five minutes to finish. Those who did finish a few minutes early were excited to begin exploring some of the insect books in our room.

Although the goal of the lesson was more to get students thinking than to have them produce a beautiful end product, they did create some elaborate pieces. Elizabeth, for example, drew with careful detail a series of insects and wrote several facts about each. Her ladybug had a speech bubble that said, "I'm a ladybug. I am an insect. I only fly when it's warm, and I have six legs!"

Reflection Phase Spurs Further Interest

The children's enthusiasm increased as they shared their projects with the group and chose which of their facts to add to our list. Our finished list was a long one. As the children surveyed it, some began to doubt whether their facts were correct, just as Joshua had done earlier.

I made a mental note for myself that the finished list contained many misconceptions. One child, for example, offered that "Wasps eat butterflies which eat gnats which eat ladybugs which eat aphids which eat mosquitoes." The list gave me a clear idea of what the children already knew about insects and what they still needed to understand.

As we finished our list of what we knew (or thought we knew), many children were already asking when they could choose an insect and begin their research projects. I overheard excited conversations about insects throughout the day. Many children took a break from their afternoon independent reading book to read some of our insect books. Joshua wanted to see if dragonfly adults had six legs or four and eagerly reported his findings at the end of independent reading time (they have six).

What Students Want to Learn

The next day, we gathered to discuss what we now wanted to learn about insects. The children had many questions. "How long do insects live?" they wanted to know. "Are there mixed-breed insects? Do wasps' stingers fall off when they sting? How and why do bees and wasps sting?" They had so many questions that I could hardly call on each of them fast enough.

As the unit progressed, students wanted to add questions to our "What we want to learn about" list. Then, when they discovered answers to some of their classmates' questions through their individual research projects, they enthusiastically shared their new knowledge.

Several children also delighted in discovering that some "facts" on our "What we know" list were incorrect. And before we ended the unit, the children wanted to make sure that we answered all the questions no one had yet addressed.

Good Teaching and Good Learning

This Academic Choice lesson accomplished two important things: First, it sparked excitement and curiosity that inspired the children's learning throughout the insect unit. Second, it guided the teachers by telling us what the children knew and what they still wanted or needed to know. In all four of our classrooms, this meant good teaching and good learning.

Open-Ended Questions
Stretching Children's Academic and Social Learning

AN ADAPTED EXCERPT FROM THE NEFC BOOK

THE POWER OF OUR WORDS: TEACHER LANGUAGE THAT HELPS

CHILDREN LEARN BY PAULA DENTON, EDD

Language is one of the most powerful tools available to teachers. We can use language to stretch children's curiosity, reasoning ability, creativity, and independence. One effective way to do this is by asking open-ended questions—those with no single right or wrong answer. Instead of predictable answers, open-ended questions elicit fresh and sometimes even startling insights and ideas, opening minds and enabling teachers and students to build knowledge together.

In this article, I give examples of open-ended questions, explain what makes them so powerful, and offer some tips on how to use these questions to bolster children's learning.

Open-Ended Questions in Action

Ms. Nunn's class is about to read a new story, and the children have opened their books to the first page. To spark their curiosity about the story, she asks a series of open-ended questions (shown here in italics) that draw out their thoughts, knowledge, and feelings.

"Before we start," Ms. Nunn says, "take a look at just this page. *What interesting words do you see?*" After a few quiet moments, hands go up.

"Castle!" shouts Raymond. "Castles are cool! I have a model castle."

"I can tell that's an important word for you, Raymond. *What clues does this word give you as to what the story might be about?*"

"Knights? Usually castles have kings and knights."

"Maybe it's a fairy tale," Keira adds.

"Hmm. Interesting," Ms. Nunn muses. *"What makes you think it might be a fairy tale?"*

After the children have shared some thoughts on the nature of fairy tales, Ms. Nunn brings them back to her original question. *"What are some other interesting words on this page?"* she asks.

"Milkmaid," offers Arnie. "What's a milkmaid?"

"Hmm, what might a milkmaid be? Any guesses?"

"My grammy tells me a story about a milkmaid. It's a girl and she works hard and she's poor."

"Oh, those might be some clues," says the teacher. *"What other clues could help us understand this word?"*

The conversation continues with the children deeply engaged. Fifteen minutes later, the group has discussed context clues, compound words, historical jobs, fairy tales versus historical fiction, gender roles, and more. The students have been prompted to think, share their knowledge, analyze information, and connect ideas. Their interest in the story has grown, and their teacher has learned a great deal about what they know. Much of this richness derived from Ms. Nunn's use of open-ended questions.

What Makes Open-Ended Questions So Powerful?

Children's learning naturally loops through a cycle of wonder, exploration, discovery, reflection, and more wonder, leading them on to increasingly complex knowledge and sophisticated thinking. The power of open-ended questions comes from the way these questions tap into that natural cycle, inviting children to pursue their own curiosity about how the world works.

Open-ended questions show children that their teachers trust them to have good ideas, think for themselves, and contribute in valuable ways. The resulting sense of autonomy, belonging, and competence leads to engagement and deep investment in classroom activities.

Tips for Crafting Open-Ended Questions

Learning any new language habit takes reflection, time, and much practice. *The Power of Our Words: Teacher Language That Helps Children Learn* offers comprehensive guidelines on how to frame open-ended questions and make them a regular part of your classroom vocabulary. Here you'll find just a taste of these guidelines.

> Open-ended questions show children that their teachers trust them to have good ideas, think for themselves, and contribute in valuable ways.

GENUINELY OPEN UP YOUR CURIOSITY ABOUT STUDENTS' THINKING

For open-ended questions to be effective, it's critical that we ask them with real curiosity about children's thinking. Once I asked some fourth graders, "How might you use the colored pencils to show what you know about butterflies?"

"You could draw a butterfly and show the different parts," one child said. Others suggested, "You could make a map of Monarch butterflies' migration paths," and "You could make a chart showing the butterfly's life cycle." Then another student offered, "You could write a story about a butterfly's life and use different colors for different times in its life."

Truly surprised by this last suggestion, I realized that if I hadn't felt and conveyed genuine curiosity in all reasoned and relevant answers, that child probably wouldn't have done the creative thinking that led to such a great idea. Because of it, students' learning was stretched and our butterfly projects were richer.

Children can tell when their teachers are genuinely interested in their ideas. If we're truly interested, over time children learn to trust that we really do want to know what and how they think. When they know this, they're more willing to reason and reflect, they gain more practice in thinking for themselves, and they gradually become more skillful, creative thinkers.

57

Suppose when I asked, "How might you use the colored pencils to show what you know about butterflies?" a child had answered, "You could pretend that the colored pencils are butterflies and make a play about them." Making such a play would have met the goals of this lesson, and in terms of the question I asked, this response is just as valid as the others. But because of the potential chaos and safety issues, having students "fly" colored pencils around the room was more than I wanted to deal with.

Fortunately, no student really gave such an answer. But the way to prevent such a response would have been first to clarify to myself the boundaries of what I wanted the children to think about, and then articulate these boundaries to the children. The resulting wording might have been "How could you use these colored pencils to draw or write something that shows what you know about butterflies?" This is still an open-ended question; it just has boundaries based on what I might see as appropriate options for a particular group of students.

USE WORDS THAT ENCOURAGE COOPERATION, NOT COMPETITION

Sometimes an open-ended question leads to competition to see who can give the best answer. Although well-managed competition has a place in certain school arenas, teachers usually use open-ended questions when the goal is for students to collaborate, to learn from and with each other, not to compete.

To keep discussions from turning into competitions, phrase your questions carefully. Competition often arises from questions beginning with "who" or "whose" ("Who knows a good way to use clay?"); using words such as "better," "best," or "most" ("How can we make this graph the most beautiful?"); or somehow elevating some students above others ("Kerry, what strategies for writing neatly can you show the class?"). These natural-seeming ways of talking assume some answers will be better than others, which encourages competition.

A simple rephrasing helps. Instead of "Who can tell me a good way to use the clay?" try "What are some good ways we could use the clay?" Replace "How can we make this graph the most beautiful?" with "What are some different ways to make this graph beautiful?"

WATCH OUT FOR PSEUDO OPEN-ENDED QUESTIONS

Pseudo open-ended questions sound open-ended but have behind them the teacher's desire for a certain answer. I once had a student who loved magenta. Everything she colored, painted, or modeled in clay prominently featured magenta.

Perhaps because I'm not crazy about magenta, or because I wanted her to buck the "girls are pink, boys are blue" stereotype, one day, seeing another magenta-infused drawing, I asked, "What do you think would happen if you used a different color?" Only when she replied, "I think I wouldn't like it as much" did I realize I had wanted her to say, "I think it would look better."

It took me a moment to resist the urge to explain my thinking and to become genuinely curious about hers. "Hmm. Why do you say that?" I managed to ask.

"This color stands out," she replied. "You can see it from far away, not like pink or yellow."

"Not like pink," I repeated to myself. I was so wrong, thinking this student was going for "girly" pink when she was going for standing out. Her explanation gave me real insight into her thinking.

Fortunately, in this instance, I caught myself after the student said "I think I wouldn't like it as much." But what if a teacher doesn't catch herself? When we fish for specific answers, children soon realize we're not really asking for their thoughts, knowledge, or perceptions, but for them to articulate our own. Many then stop thinking and become less engaged. Or they respond by guessing wildly at the answer the teacher wants. Except for the child who guesses correctly, the children—and their teacher—will likely feel discouraged after such an interaction. Not much will have been learned, or taught. All would have turned out differently if the question had been truly open-ended and the teacher's intention truly to hear what the children thought.

Leading the Way to True Learning

Open-ended questions power academic and social learning. Such questions encourage children's natural curiosity, challenging them to think for themselves, and inviting them to share their view of the world. The result: engaged learners who are motivated to learn and whose responses enlighten their classmates and their teacher.

Focusing ᴼᴺ ᵀᴴᴱ Schoolwide Community

Peace on the Playground
Teaching Care, Friendliness, and Cooperation

BY MARLYNN K. CLAYTON

Group games should be a positive experience for all children, not just the "winners" and the "most athletic." Win or lose, each participant should enjoy the benefits of physical challenge, exercise, problem-solving, and strategic thinking.

Group play also offers children opportunities to enhance self-esteem, develop a sense of belonging, learn cooperative skills, identify with a group, and commit to goals, all of which contribute to academic success.

Of course, group play should also be fun!

All of this doesn't just happen on the playground. Instead, teachers need to systematically teach children how to play hard in friendly, cooperative, and caring ways. Teaching children how to play is just as important as teaching them how to read.

This article outlines steps that enable virtually all children to enthusiastically participate in cooperative outside play.

Introducing Game-Playing

Children's discovery of the benefits of group play begins in the classroom. Start with a discussion, with children seated in a circle.

The discussion has two objectives: first, to motivate and excite the children; second, to establish basic rules for safe, friendly play.

For example, you might begin a brainstorming session by saying, "This year, we will play many games together, inside and outside. Why do you think we play games?"

Use a class chart to enter children's responses, which typically include "to have fun" or "to have a good time." Introduce these concepts yourself if the children don't name them.

Next, you might say, "My goal for our play is for everyone to have fun, but I also want everyone to be safe. How can we take care of ourselves and each other so that everyone is safe and has fun?" Again, use a chart to record responses. Here's a list of ideas that you should eventually address:

* Follow the rules of the game.

* Stay within boundaries.

* Help others (e.g., those who fall down, are less skilled, or make mistakes).

* Include everyone.

* Use safe walking, running, and tagging.

* Follow the teacher's signals.

* Congratulate players on the losing team.

Teaching Rules

There are five rules to explicitly teach in the classroom before the first outdoor play session.

RULE #1: FOLLOW TEACHER'S SIGNALS

Model for children the signals you will use on the playground to get their attention and to ensure safety. For example:

* Hands up. The teacher raises her or his hand for quiet and attention. Children respond by becoming quiet, looking at the teacher, and raising their hands to spread the signal.

* "Freeze." Children freeze in place when they hear this signal.

* "Circle up." Children form a circle with the teacher.

* "Alee. Alee." Children come from anywhere on the playground to circle up or line up at an agreed-upon spot when they hear this call from the teacher.

Feel free to create your own calls and signals. Explain the purpose of each signal, and model each one.

RULE #2: WALK AND RUN SAFELY

Start by asking, "Who can show us how to walk safely?" and have a child demonstrate. Then ask, "What about two people walking together?" Proceed to three people, four, and so on, until everyone is walking safely. Then use "Freeze."

Proceed to running. Have children show safe running with one, two, and possibly three children. (Classroom space may limit the number of children who can demonstrate safe running at one time.)

RULE #3: STAY WITHIN BOUNDARIES

Create a simple boundary on the floor using rope or a piece of furniture. "Here's a boundary. Who can show us how to stay within the boundary while walking? While running?"

"What can we do when someone falls down when walking or running? Who thinks they can show us?" Have children role-play appropriate behavior.

"Who thinks they can show us a safe way to line up when the game is over?" Again, have children demonstrate proper behavior.

Practicing the Rules Outside

Next, take the children outside to practice all the rules you taught inside. Have children demonstrate the rules in "game" form so that practice is fun.

For example, after walking the boundaries, play the Freeze Game. Children stay within the boundaries and walk, run, twirl, hop, etc., until they hear "Freeze!" They stay frozen until they hear the cue ("Melt," "Go for it," etc.) to become active again.

An extension to the Freeze Game is the Command Game, in which children walk, run, twirl, hop, and so on, until they hear "Freeze," "Circle up," or "Alee. Alee."

When a round is over, gather children together. Allow them to share something they learned and what they liked about the game. Then comments on the positive behavior you observed.

Teaching "Advanced" Rules

Next, move on teaching more subtle rules, which are often more challenging for children to follow. Always introduce these concepts before they become issues during actual play. Concepts to include:

* Choosing teams so that everyone feels good

* Including everyone

* Helping others

* Boosting the spirits of losing team members

Create practice games that allow children to learn these advanced rules. For example, "Show how to tag three people before I count to ten," you might say. This ensures that children include many classmates instead of simply chasing a best friend. Try to make up noncompetitive games in which children feel no pressure to win or lose.

66

Teaching New Games

It's important for the teacher to teach specific rules and techniques when introducing any new game. Tag games are a prime example.

The first concept to teach in tag is safe and careful tagging. Start by asking, "How can we tag someone in a safe, careful, and friendly way?" Explain and demonstrate that a safe tag is a gentle one, on the shoulder or back; then have children demonstrate a safe tag.

Other concepts to teach for tag games include:

* "Tagger's Choice"—The tagger is always right, even if his or her tag was so soft that it wasn't felt.

* "Limited Time on Safety"—Children must count to five or ten and then leave.

* "No Babysitting"—A tagger must stand five paces away from safety while the "safe" child counts to five or ten.

Children do best when lots of them are taggers, when they play short games, and when the game ends before only one person is left untagged.

The Importance of Practice

Before outside play, always review the rules of the day's game, and include brief modeling when necessary. Then, before beginning actual play, allow plenty of time for "no pressure" practice. This allows children to build competency and mastery by simulating game situations.

To maintain interest and enthusiasm, continue to introduce new games to children, complete with modeling and practice before actual play. During the school year, slowly build a repertoire of familiar games.

Reflecting on the Play Experience

Following the first few outdoor play periods, allow time for indoor discussions. These sessions enable children to share reflections of the play experience and to comment on what they learned and enjoyed about each game. It's also important for you to continue reinforcement of the positive behavior you observed on the playground.

Sometimes children will share negative play experiences with the group. In these situations, encourage children to establish safe, nonthreatening ways to discuss and solve problems.

If you encounter more serious problems associated with individual children, discuss them privately with those involved. Conclude "problem" discussions by reflecting on positive parts of the game.

WHOLE-SCHOOL RECESS

These same techniques and strategies encourage safety and cooperation when playing games during general recess time. However, for these methods to work at recess, your school staff must agree philosophically on the goals, management signals, and structures for play.

Staff members must commit to spending extra time and effort to teaching children appropriate behavior on the playground during the first few weeks of school. Also, during these first few weeks, always choose games that are noncompetitive, non-eliminating, and focused on group-building.

These four steps can help ensure a peaceful playground during recess:

Week 1: Begin with your own class.

Each teacher begins introducing and teaching outside play to his or her own class, using the guidelines presented earlier. Recess staff pair up with classroom teachers.

Week 2: Proceed to group play.

Place children into several small groups that will remain together during the second week. Each recess staff member manages a different game. Rotate groups among staff members so that children learn many games. It's best if classroom teachers participate in games to model and reinforce appropriate behavior.

Week 3: Mix groups and continue group play. Recess staff work alone.

Establish new play groups that will stay together for the third week. Rotate groups through the recess staff as in Week 2. Introduce new games, if desired. Classroom teachers help when necessary.

Tips for Promoting Safe, Caring Play throughout the Year

Use positive language.

Positive language promotes positive behavior. A teacher's language should empower children and encourage them to practice positive behavior.

Focus on noncompetitive, non-elimination games.

Children have more fun and feel better when they actively participate in most or all of a game instead of being eliminated and watching others play. Noncompetitive games help children focus on the fun part of games. Most children enjoy games more when not thinking about winning or losing.

Troubleshoot.

Most games have potential trouble spots. For example, in tag, some children may tag too aggressively. Anticipate trouble spots and plan ahead. Model and role-play appropriate behavior before trouble occurs.

Observe carefully. Stop play when necessary.

You can't anticipate every trouble spot, so once play begins, watch for problem situations. If a situation demands immediate attention, stop the play and, if appropriate, encourage the group to help solve the problem. For example, you might ask, "What do you think is the best thing to do in a situation like this?" (Expect a lot of stop points during the first few weeks of school.) For less troublesome incidents, take note of the situation and role-play appropriate behavior later.

Use time-out for small problems.

Once rules have been established and successfully practiced, use time-out for minor problems. This helps check inappropriate behavior before a situation gets out of control.

Week 4 and beyond: Allow children to choose their games.

When all children know the repertoire of games and demonstrate friendly, caring playground behavior, let them choose which games to play. Recess staff can offer a selection of games from which to choose, or children can make their own suggestions. The important thing is to let the children decide. Staff may set a limit for the number of participants in each game, and then ask children to make a second choice.

Continue to introduce new games throughout the year, but always make sure that all children learn each game. You can vary your groupings of children—by age, by classroom, and so on. Keep in mind, however, that mixed-age groups work best; they tend to suppress ultra-competitive instincts. Throughout the process, recess staff must take care to follow and reinforce the techniques and strategies discussed earlier.

The Middle of the Day

BY GAIL HEALY

I t's a cool, crisp, autumn morning as a hundred second and third graders burst onto the playground for a much-needed break from the academic demands of the day. Some make a beeline to a kickball game starting up in a far corner of the playground with the "recess/lunch teacher" serving as pitcher and referee. Others dart to the play structure supervised by an instructional aide. In mid-field, a lively round of relay races starts to take shape with the help of two fifth grade peer mediators. In yet another corner of the field, a game of "Cut the Cake," led by a special education teacher, quickly grows from a group of three to a group of twenty-three. Children move in and out of games with ease. There are no lengthy debates about rules, no fights about who can play, no tears. There are no children wandering aimlessly about, and for those who prefer a quieter break in the day, there is a supply of books, paper, and markers under a nearby maple tree. It's an active, playful, and peaceful twenty-five minutes, and children and adults leave it feeling refreshed and relaxed.

While this scenario may sound too good to be true, it's actually a fairly typical fall recess at our school. It's the result of a concerted effort that began two years ago to address the recurring conflicts and tensions that surfaced daily during recess and lunch.

During previous years, we had worked hard as a whole staff to improve the learning climate in our school. While we had made great strides, one part of the day—the midday recess/lunchtime—remained problematic.

70

Not only was recess filled with conflicts that inevitably made their way back into the classroom, but many students simply had no idea what to do during this time. Hesitant to join one of the highly competitive and physical games that typically dominated recess, they wandered aimlessly around the playground, interacting with no one. The resulting feelings of alienation often led to conflicts later in the day.

Lunchtime was not much better. It was noisy and chaotic and filled with mishaps. Children often felt excluded, and there was a glaring lack of consistency between the expectations in the classroom and those in the lunchroom.

Adults were spending far too much time writing and sending home discipline notes, and everyone—teachers, parents, and students—felt frustrated. Our staff decided that it was time to confront the problems. Here's how we approached them.

Phase One: Getting Started

During the first year, we reflected on the problems, explored possible solutions, and took a few initial steps toward improving recess and lunch.

REORDERING THE MIDDLE OF THE DAY

One of the first changes we made was to reverse the order of recess and lunch so that children went outside and played before coming inside to eat. In his book *Time to Teach, Time to Learn*, Chip Wood, Northeast Foundation for Children co-founder, urges schools to make this change because of his belief that eating first and then going out to play is "disruptive to both the educational system and the digestive system. Better to work up an appetite with exercise, come in to eat, settle down, and take a rest."

After making this change for two out of the three recess/lunch periods (schedule constraints prevented changing the third), teachers immediately noticed a positive change in students' emotions and demeanor when they reentered the classroom after lunch. Also, there were fewer conflicts in the lunchroom and on the playground, and those that occurred were mediated more quickly.

IMPROVING K–1 RECESS FIRST

At the same time, we began having whole-staff brainstorms about recess and lunch: How could we structure recess to make it more enjoyable and safe for all students? How could we make lunch calmer and more relaxing for everyone?

As a first step, we decided to focus on improving the kindergarten/first grade recess. The plan was to increase the number of adults on the playground and to give them more active roles.

Previously there were two adults on the playground and their involvement was limited to intervening when problems arose. Now there would be four adults, and each one would lead a different game or activity that students would be required to either participate in or watch.

While we didn't have the funds to hire two additional staff members for recess, we were able to make changes in our schedules so that two instructional assistants could be at recess in addition to the two paraprofessionals already there. I also made an effort to be there whenever possible, as did the behavior management teacher. After trying this plan for a few weeks, there was such a dramatic improvement in the quality of play and social interactions that we knew we were on the right track.

Phase Two: Taking It to the Next Step

Encouraged by these early successes and eager for more widespread improvements, I made contact over the summer with all the adults who would be involved with recess and lunch. I shared my excitement about further improving this time of the day and invited their input. This group met before school began to solidify plans and to prepare for the first days of school. Here are the key ideas we set into motion at the beginning of the year.

A CHANGE IN TITLE

We felt it was important to change the titles of certain members of the group from "paraprofessionals" to "recess/lunch teachers." This title more accurately reflected their role and our belief that, in the words of Chip Wood, "teaching recess and lunch is just as important as teaching reading and math." Additional members of the group, including the behavior management teacher and several instructional aides, also began to see themselves as "recess/lunch teachers" during the middle of the day.

TEACHING GAMES

In the first week of school, recess/lunch teachers were paired with individual classes, grades K–5, during recess. The adults taught one game a day. We chose games that encouraged cooperation and could be played independently by the students. Every student was expected either to participate actively or to keenly observe the games.

During this stage, I received several phone calls from concerned parents who wondered why their child "didn't have recess anymore" or "had to play a game during recess."

I addressed these concerns as they arose, and I also included information in our September and October parent newsletters explaining our rationale and plans for teaching recess and lunch. For the most part, families were very supportive of this new approach.

OPENING OF THE PLAY STRUCTURE

At the same time that games were being taught on the playground, we were teaching individual classes how to use and care for the play structure.

At the start of the school year, the play structure was wrapped in orange construction tape with a large CLOSED sign hanging in the center. Each day a different class was chosen to do an exploration of the structure led by one of the recess/ lunch teachers. Each part of the structure was explored, its potential uses discussed, demonstrated, and practiced. Rules for safety were talked about, written up, and sent to every staff member and classroom. The structure was opened once this was done with every class.

TEACHING LUNCH

During the first four days of school, classroom teachers accompanied their classes to the cafeteria in the morning to practice lunch. Several recess/lunch teachers were present, including myself, to explain and model everything from lunchroom procedures—such as where to go to get your lunch, what to take when you get there, what to do if you forget something—to table manners, including where and how to sit at

> While our ultimate goal was for the children to increase their independence during recess and lunch, we were careful not to pull out support too soon.

tables and what you might want to talk about. Not only did children enjoy this modeling, but it also made an immediate positive impact on their behavior at lunch.

REFLECTING AND REVISING

Then, every Friday, the recess/lunch team met to talk about how things were going and to make changes as needed. Should there be more supervision? Less supervision? While our ultimate goal was for the children to increase their independence during recess and lunch, we were careful not to pull out support too soon.

By the end of the second week of school, we all agreed that the fourth/fifth grade recess was running smoothly. While there was still some adult involvement in the games, the children were for the most part organizing their own games and doing so in a friendly and inclusive way.

Several weeks later, we felt that the second/third grade recess was also ready for more independence. We began by offering them a "choice" day on Fridays, when children practiced leading games and had access to recess equipment such as jump ropes and balls. Student mediators, who had been participating in the games up to this point, were now being asked to lead them. Meanwhile, we decided not to make any changes in the kindergarten/first grade recess for the time being. The high degree of adult involvement still seemed essential for this younger group.

Many people notice that lunch is calmer and recess more peaceful this year. Teachers comment that there is greater consistency in the rules throughout the school. Perhaps most importantly, children seem more relaxed during recess and lunch. Because of this, the middle of the day truly does offer a break from the demands of academics. It's a time for children to rest and recharge. When they return to the classroom, they are ready to learn. It has taken a strong team effort to reach this point, an effort that everyone agrees has been well worth the time and energy.

Success Night

A Year-End Celebration of All Students' Accomplishments

AN ADAPTED EXCERPT FROM NEFC'S BOOK
IN OUR SCHOOL: BUILDING COMMUNITY IN ELEMENTARY SCHOOLS
BY KAREN L. CASTO, EDD, AND JENNIFER R. AUDLEY

*W*hen Kyle and his grandparents walk into Summit *Elementary School on Success Night, the hallways are already buzzing with children and their families. Kyle's grandmother catches sight of his second grade teacher and waves. Kyle says they'll visit her room later. "First I'm going to show you what I've done this year," he explains as he steers his family down the hallway toward his fifth grade classroom.*

Success Night, held on an evening in May, is the most popular family event of the year at Summit Elementary, a preK–6 school in Cincinnati, Ohio. This year-end celebration of all students' accomplishments gives every child an opportunity to shine before families, teachers, and peers.

At Summit, this event has replaced the traditional year-end awards ceremony,

which singled out some students and left others unrecognized. Success Night is both a more inclusive and a more positive way to end the school year. Fifth grade teacher Lisa Courtney explains, "With Success Night, students describe their achievements in their own words, and the focus is on celebrating growth and being proud, which applies to everyone."

Every student in the school participates by creating a display highlighting his or her proudest accomplishments for the year. On the night itself, hundreds of family members attend the celebration. Most families spend the first forty-five minutes in their child's classroom and then an equal amount of time visiting other classrooms. After the first half of the evening, teachers leave their classrooms so they, too, can see the student work shown throughout the building. "The hallways and classrooms are just decorated to the max with children's work and reflections," says kindergarten teacher Katie Geiger. "It's the end of the year, but it's so clear that learning is still going on."

Projects Customized by Class

Although they all share the common goal of having students reflect on and represent their accomplishments from the year, classes prepare for Success Night differently. Teachers connect this work to curriculum and current issues in their students' lives.

A KINDERGARTEN EXAMPLE:
SEE HOW MUCH WE'VE GROWN

Katie Geiger integrates her class's build-up to Success Night with preparing the children for their move from a half-day, mostly self-contained kindergarten experience to a full-length school day in first grade.

She begins by showing the children the pictures they'd drawn and sentences they'd dictated back in September to describe their hopes for their kindergarten year. At this age, the children's hopes are usually quite simple and concrete. For example, they might have said they hoped to take care of a class pet, or to hear lots of stories. Ms. Geiger asks students to think about whether they accomplished their goals. However, she explains, this exercise is about more than seeing if their hopes came true: "It also gets children thinking about how much they've grown. When I show them these and other samples of their work from earlier in the year, they can't believe how they used to do things."

Photographs courtesy of Summit Elementary School

At the end of this process, each child makes a poster highlighting something she or he feels especially proud of having done in kindergarten. These posters are displayed in the classroom on Success Night.

When visitors arrive on Success Night, Ms. Geiger provides each family with a list of things they might do together during the evening. All of the evening's events help students and their families look forward to first grade with confidence. Activities in the classroom, such as reading a favorite book, looking through journals, and admiring the posters, spotlight the students' accomplishments and readiness for first grade learning. Other activities, such as visiting first grade and special areas classrooms, allow children to demonstrate their ability to navigate the school building.

Students are asked to reflect on their growth in four areas: academics, athletics, creative pursuits, and citizenship.

A FIFTH GRADE EXAMPLE: ESSAYS WITH ACCOMPANYING EVIDENCE

For older students, such as those in Lisa Courtney's fifth grade class, Success Night is the culmination of a reflective process that begins in April with preparation for state-wide testing. First, teachers focus on reviewing academic topics covered in fifth grade.

Then, after testing is complete, they ask students to reflect on their growth in four areas: academics, athletics, creative pursuits, and citizenship. Each fifth grader selects an accomplishment in one of those areas to describe in writing and support with evidence. Their essays and the accompanying evidence—such as certificates, notes from teachers, work samples, and objects—are displayed on their desks on Success Night. Families are invited first to look at their child's work, then to peruse classmates' work, and finally to visit other grade levels and specials teachers' rooms.

SPECIALS ROOM DISPLAYS

Special area classrooms also have displays on Success Night. These rooms showcase student products and processes from the year in their respective subjects. Specials teachers tend to use the first forty-five minutes, when almost all students and parents are in their homerooms, to travel through the building, see classroom displays, and connect with students. They then return to their "home bases" for the second half of the evening, which is when most parents and students come to visit them.

Community-Building an Added Benefit

Success Night not only provides parents, grandparents, and other family members with an opportunity to learn about their own children's accomplishments, it increases families' sense of connection to the school as a whole. With teachers, students, and their families intermingled throughout the school, all learning about student accomplishments across grades, "it feels like a celebration of all of us," says Lisa Courtney.

Success Night also helps people in the school deepen their knowledge of each other, which is as important at the end of the year as at the beginning. By seeing students' displays in the hallways and reading students' reflections on their accomplishments in a variety of areas, teachers and classmates learn about children's talents, interests, news, and growth. Many classes make games for Success Night that build on this theme. For instance, first grade classes make posters with a question written on a flap ("Guess who got a baby brother this year?"). Players make a guess and then check their answer by lifting up the flap to see a child's photo and name.

A Beloved Ten-Year Tradition

It's been a decade since Summit Elementary began Success Night. Over the years the school has fine-tuned the year-end event, from finding simple ways to make displays more effective (for example, leaving folders containing student work open rather than closed) to having students practice being guides for their families beforehand. The result, ten years later, is a smooth-running all-school tradition that celebrates all students and is universally beloved.

Working WITH Families

Reaching Out to Parents

BY CHIP WOOD AND MARY BETH FORTON

A healthy partnership between school and family is one of the most powerful unions teachers can help create. We have found that the energy we put into helping parents feel informed about and involved in their child's life at school yields enormous dividends.

Although there are many things a teacher can do throughout the school year to encourage a strong and productive relationship with parents, the beginning of the school year presents a natural opportunity to begin this process. It is a time when both teachers and parents are focused on hopes for their children's year. In this article, we'll outline methods we find effective for initiating a parent-teacher partnership based on cooperation and trust.

The First Contact

The first step is to reach out to parents as soon as possible. Rather than waiting until November, scheduling the first parent-teacher conference during the early weeks of school helps teachers develop a solid relationship with parents. Not only is the information exchanged at such a conference helpful, but it also creates a positive context that makes it easier to communicate about issues and problems that arise during the year.

Sample Parent Conference Letter

Dear Parents,

This year we will be doing our parent-teacher conferences differently than we have in the past. I feel very excited about these changes.

First of all, we will hold our first conference much earlier in the school year. This will allow teachers to get to know parents sooner and to learn more about our students. I believe this will strengthen the connection and greatly improve the communication between home and school.

At this first conference, I will be asking you to talk about your hopes for your child's school year. Specifically, I would like to know what you think is most important for your child to learn in school this year. Please choose one goal that you would like us to focus on. I will be paying careful attention to this goal and documenting growth in this area. At mid-year, we'll evaluate your child's progress in this area and decide whether to continue with this goal or, if the goal is accomplished, to choose another.

During this first conference, I will also share with you my plans and goals for this school year and answer any questions you may have. I'm looking forward to working together with you to make this a wonderful year of learning for your child.

Sincerely,

Mary Beth Forton

Inviting Parent Input

A powerful way to open the dialogue with parents is to begin the conference by asking "What do you think is most important for your child to learn this year?" Not only does this question engage the parents immediately in a meaningful way, but it sets a tone of collaboration, and the answers give us important insights into our new students.

Some teachers send a letter home prior to this meeting to give parents time to think about their goal for their child (see sample letter). The parents' response in the conference then provides a point of interest with which to start this conversation between parents and teacher.

Responding to Parent Goals

"I'm worried about his math skills," shares Martin's father. "Shouldn't he know his times tables by now?" As we listen to his concern and note the goal, we might also follow this up by telling him what our plans are for this year's math program.

At this initial conference we use a form that both parent and teacher can keep to document the goal. This form serves as our reminder and assures parents that we have heard and understood their goal. It is an important reference as we monitor the work of the child in this area, and we refer to this goal in future communications with parents and on report cards. To give the process meaning and purpose, we let parents know from the start that we plan to document progress in the goal area. We want them to know that we really care about their goal and will be paying attention to it throughout the year. We try to save tangible evidence that shows the child's progress in this area, evidence that we can show to parents and include in a child's portfolio or simply share with child and parent as a measure of growth.

Although many parent goals focus on academic progress, some parents wonder about social goals. "I think Robin is doing just fine with her schoolwork," a parent says, "but what I'd really like her to do this year is to make some friends."

> Scheduling the first parent-teacher conference during the early weeks of school helps teachers develop a solid relationship with parents.

83

If we see the issue named as one that we're able and willing to work on with the child, we ask parents at this point if this is the area they'd like us to focus on with their child for the year. In this example where the goal involves social skills, documentation of growth may include photographs of the child working or playing with a friend, a story the child wrote about a friend, or teacher-written observations of the child in social situations.

Sharing Your Hopes and Goals

After the parent goal has been established and discussed, it is a good time to talk about our hopes and goals for the class and the student this year. The process of discussing each other's goals for the year allows teachers and parents to think aloud together and to understand each other's point of view. Sharing information is a vital part of the foundation upon which parents' investment and involvement will be built.

While most parents bring a lifetime of knowledge about their children to the conference, we usually have much less. Yet it is important to feel that we really know a child well enough to formulate a goal for her. Sometimes a prior year's records or a chat with last year's teacher informs us. When we do get information about the child from previous teachers, we often ask parents about their perceptions. For example, past teachers may have commented that a child is easily distracted and can't concentrate on work. We've found it helpful to raise the issue with parents before a problem has developed in this year's classroom and teachers and parents feel strained or defensive. It can be illuminating to find out what the parents' thoughts are. Do they have a different perception? Do they know of some strategies that could be helpful to their child and teacher? Are they looking for help with this issue?

From *Teaching Children to Care*

by Ruth Sidney Charney, published by Northeast Foundation for Children

Our school schedules a pre-school and late-fall conference. At the first conference, parents are asked to think about their priorities for their child. "What do you feel is most important for your child to work on this year in school?" Often the parents share compelling insights, pertinent history, lingering anxieties, and deep aspirations. We find out about children's interests, habits, attitudes, and struggles.

We are all sometimes afraid for our children, fearful that, lacking certain accomplishments, they will not hold their own in the world. These worries and hopes can produce a flood of demands on top of existing teaching prescriptions that assess and measure numerous discrete skills. If we are not careful, we start the year preparing for a marathon. When we ask ourselves and parents, "What is most important?" we intend to shorten the list and highlight a plan. The more we identify a focus, the better able we are to devote attention and effort to a course of improvement. And the more tangible successes children experience, and parents and teachers witness, the more pride and hope we create.

Children are responsive to the concerns and expectations issued by their parents and teachers. "I don't like the math we are doing right now," explained Tyrone, "but I know it's important for me." He "knows" because his parents have emphasized his need to improve his accuracy and proficiency with operations. He cares, not because the material provides intrinsic satisfaction or interest, but because of his authentic desire to please.

Of course, these conferences will not always run smoothly. Some parents don't show up or respond to our letters. We must leave the door open to these parents, perhaps sending them a follow-up letter telling them we missed them, letting them know what our goals are for their child or the class, inviting them to add their own goal either through a note or phone conversation.

Handling Unrealistic Goals

Occasionally we encounter parents who choose a goal that we know is unrealistic for their child. At this point in the year, we try to acknowledge the positive in the goal. We try not to contest it or to come across as the expert, which may put the parents on the defensive. We remind ourselves that the purpose of this conference is to understand and communicate and to establish a warm working relationship with parents.

So, for instance, when the parents of a first-grader tell us that they want their child to be able to read Hardy Boys books by December, we might respond by acknowledging the parents' interest in their child's reading progress and by talking about our reading program this year. The goal can be paraphrased on the form as "Parents want Jamie to get better at reading."

Parents may change their goal as the year progresses. Some goals may be accomplished in two months; some may take two years. At some point close to the middle of the year (at our next conference or in a letter attached to the mid-year report card), we like to check in with parents by asking them, "How do you think your child is doing in meeting the goal?" and "Has your goal for your child changed?" The feedback we receive gives us valuable information and lets us know whether our perceptions of the children match the parents' perceptions.

Family Inventory

In addition to this September parent conference, we like to send out a Family Inventory at the beginning of the school year as a way to establish a connection with families and to welcome parents and grandparents into the classroom.

In this inventory, parents and grandparents are asked if they would be willing to volunteer some of their time in the classroom. The inventory asks them to list any special talents, skills, interests, or cultural traditions that they would be willing to share. This offers a way to learn about our students' families, to help parents and grandparents feel welcome, and to bring rich resources into the curriculum.

Parents as partners in the education of their child widen the potential for the growth of every child. Inventories, conferences, and goal-setting all help enlist parents and let parents know that we, as teachers, wish their help. When parents feel this welcome into their child's classroom, warm and collaborative teacher-parent relationships are possible and form a rich foundation for work with the child during the year.

Editor's note: For more ideas on working with families, see *Parents and Teachers Working Together* by Carol Davis and Alice Yang, published by Northeast Foundation for Children.

Wonderful Wednesdays

Inviting Parents into Our Classroom Community

BY CALTHA CROWE

Morning Meeting is over in our third grade classroom, and writing workshop is underway. The children are scattered around the room sketching and then writing about objects that "called out to them." Erin's dad is leaning against the file cabinet, absorbed as he sketches a ceramic rooster. Lauren's mom is quietly bouncing baby Amy on her knee as she writes down her thoughts.

I ring the chime, signaling the group to come to the rug for group sharing. We go around the circle, and everyone who wants to reads a favorite line from his/her writing. Erin's dad, Phil, says, "Thank you for inviting me to be part of this beautiful morning. Here's something I wrote: 'The rooster crows, its feathers glowing red, yellow, and blue against the alabaster egg.'"

Phil, an artist, was never comfortable in school. Today, his relaxed and engaged participation in the sketching, writing, and sharing indicates a newfound easiness with school and hints at a beginning understanding of the power that such activities have in deepening his daughter's learning.

For a number of years now I've invited parents into my classroom for these weekly or biweekly open houses, which we call Wonderful Wednesdays. I keep these days structured around workshop-type activities and ask parents to join us as full participants. They're not there to be helpers or passive observers. They aren't there to see a show or to be the show. Rather, the purpose is for parents to experience day-to-day life in our classroom in a safe and comfortable way.

Helping Parents Understand Today's Classroom

Classrooms today are often so different from those of a generation ago. When most of my students' parents think of reading, writing, spelling, and math, they probably don't picture the workshop setting, or practice through games and fun, or choice in academic activities—all of which are routine parts of their children's school day. An important goal of Wonderful Wednesdays, then, is to allow parents to understand these approaches by participating in them, by laughing with us and thinking hard with us, by experiencing that delicate balance of low stress and high rigor that we achieve at our best moments.

Caltha Crowe

One Wednesday, Gretchen's mom came. Gretchen is a precocious child with exceptional number sense. Her mother had said to me that she was sure our math program wasn't challenging enough for her daughter. That day, the children brainstormed ideas for math choice and then set off to do their chosen activities. Gretchen, a classmate Katie, and their two moms were soon engrossed in a game of Target.

As they finished the game, Gretchen's mom said, "I really had to think." I believe she got a glimpse of how school is both fun and rigorous, and of how her daughter is allowed to work at the appropriate level of challenge for her.

A Way for Me to Get to Know Parents

The school-home connection is a two-way street. It's just as important for me to know parents as it is for parents to know our classroom and my teaching approach. I teach in a large school in a busy community where it can be hard to establish tight connections with families. Even so, I think that through Wonderful Wednesdays I have been able to attain a measure of familiarity and rapport with many of them. This connection not only makes my work more enjoyable, but it is essential to my work, for in order to teach my students well, I need to know something of their life outside of school.

For example, Mike's writing is full of creative ideas but equally full of spelling and punctuation mistakes. His older brother, Toby, who was in my class last year, worried over every detail of his writing and produced polished, clean pieces. As I watch their mother, Lynne, in our classroom, I see that she is more like Toby, something of a perfectionist. When Lynne responds to a letter that Mike writes to her by covering it with red marks, I am able to keep the family picture in mind and avoid becoming irritated with Lynne. I set up a conference with her to discuss ways that we can collaborate to help Mike develop his unique talents as well as help him meet minimum standards for clean writing.

Relaxed Participation, Realistic View

Since Wonderful Wednesdays go on for most of the year, and parents can come as few or as many times as they'd like, there are usually only a small number of parents in the classroom on any given Wednesday.

Tips for Success

Wait until the classroom community feels solid before starting. This might be around October or November. The goal is for parents to feel the power of a caring and rigorous learning environment, a goal best achieved once the community is strong.

Announce dates for the year in the initial invitation. The dates, even if they're tentative, allow parents to plan ahead.

Maintain a predictable schedule on Wonderful Wednesdays. For example, in our class, math academic choice is at 10:15 every Wonderful Wednesday, and the Cherry Pie spelling game is always at 12:45. I include the schedule in the initial invitation. Parents can then join us for a subject that they feel comfortable with.

Plan activities that relate to building classroom community. Because a goal is to help parents understand our class's emphasis on cooperative learning, I save math quizzes and even guided reading groups for another day.

Clearly ask that parents participate. I say "Come as frequently or as infrequently as you please. All we ask is that you join us as a participant in our activities."

Explain that no parent has to perform. I'm careful to explain that participating is not the same as performing and that no one is expected to perform. I tell parents, for example, that they might read their own book alongside their child, but they won't be asked to read it aloud in front of the class.

Don't do Wonderful Wednesdays on days with specials. Wonderful Wednesdays in our class don't include music, PE, or other specials. It just doesn't feel collegial to announce to my colleagues that some of my students' parents will be joining their class every other Wednesday. Wonderful Wednesdays include time in our classroom only.

The rewards of involving parents through Wonderful Wednesdays pay off all year long.

Moreover, Wonderful Wednesdays are drop-in events. I don't ask parents to tell me ahead of time when they're coming. Some take the afternoon off from work or other commitments. Others stop by during their lunch hour. Some come by for Morning Meeting before they head off for their day. Whether or not we have parents join us, whether they stay for ten minutes or two hours, the class goes on with its day as usual, and any parents present simply join in the activities.

All this means that the parents, the children, and I can all get to know each other and learn with each other in a more relaxed way than at formal gatherings such as conferences or back-to-school night. Parents also get a more realistic feel for what it's like to be a student in our classroom.

A Foundation for Further Cooperation

The rewards of involving parents through Wonderful Wednesdays pay off all year long. Ray is a student who has trouble controlling his body. The other children avoid him, afraid that his rough movements will hurt them. When I discuss this with Ray's mother, our conversation goes more smoothly because of a level of trust that we have built through our contact on several Wonderful Wednesdays. She knows that I like Ray and that our community is a safe place where Ray feels like he belongs. She tells me she's eager to work with me to help Ray learn to control his body and be more accepted by his classmates.

Start Small, Then Build

If you want to try something like Wonderful Wednesdays, you might want to start small, maybe doing it just once. If the event is a success, do it again. Then add more days until having parents learning alongside their children becomes a regular feature of your classroom.

Managing Challenging Behaviors

Punishment vs. Logical Consequences

What's the Difference?

BY NEFC STAFF

Logical consequences are directly related to children's behaviors and help them fix their mistakes.

The use of logical consequences is one part of the *Responsive Classroom* approach to discipline. It's a powerful way of responding to children's misbehavior that not only is effective in stopping the behavior but is respectful of children and helps them to take responsibility for their actions.

Teachers often ask, "How are logical consequences any different from punishment?" It is a critical question because there are some basic and important differences between the two—differences that must be understood in order to use logical consequences well. Take the following example:

Six-year-old Jacob is zooming around the classroom when suddenly he trips and falls into Michelle's block building. Michelle lets out a scream, and the teacher comes over.

This first scenario involves a teacher who uses punishment. Feeling irritated, the teacher looks at Jacob and says loudly in front of the other children, "I have told you over and over again not to run in this classroom. Now see what you've done with your carelessness. Go sit in that chair and don't move until it's time for lunch."

What might be going on for Jacob? He might be thinking, "I wasn't even running. The teacher doesn't know what she's talking about. She's always picking on me. Now everybody's looking at me. I hate this school. It was a stupid building anyway."

Now, here's what might happen with a teacher who uses logical consequences. The teacher, although also feeling irritated, takes a deep breath and makes herself begin by describing what she sees: "Michelle is very upset right now because Jacob knocked over her building. I need to talk with Jacob first and then we'll figure out how to help Michelle."

The teacher takes Jacob aside and begins by asking him a question.

"What happened?"

"I just tripped and fell into it accidentally. I didn't mean to knock it over."

"Hmmm. So it was an accident. I did notice that you were running before it happened. Could that have been why you fell?"

"Maybe."

"When kids run in the classroom, accidents often happen. That's why our rule says to be safe. What do you think you could do to help Michelle?"

"I don't know."

"Maybe she would like some help putting the building back up."

Jacob nods and the teacher walks back with him to the block area. Michelle accepts Jacob's offer to help, and together they build for the rest of the period.

Now, what might be going on for Jacob? He might be learning, "When I knock things down, I have to help build them back up. I can fix things when I mess up. My teacher helps me solve problems. I have to remember to walk in the block area."

Here are some of the fundamental differences in the two approaches:

The goal of punishment is to enforce compliance with the rules by using external controls or authoritarian discipline.

* While effective in stopping the misbehavior of the moment, punishment does little to increase student responsibility.

* Punishment often leads to feelings of anger, discouragement, and resentment and an increase in evasion and deception.

The goal of logical consequences is to help children develop internal understanding, self-control, and a desire to follow the rules.

* Logical consequences help children look more closely at their behaviors and consider the results of their choices.

* Unlike punishment, where the intention is to make a child feel shamed, the intention of logical consequences is to help children develop internal controls and to learn from their mistakes in a supportive atmosphere.

Logical consequences are respectful of the child's dignity while punishment often calls upon an element of shame.

* Logical consequences respond to the misbehavior in ways that preserve the dignity of the child. The message is that the behavior is a problem, not that the child is a problem.

* The teacher's tone of voice is critical in distinguishing logical consequences from punishment. There are many ways to say to children that they've spilled their juice and should clean it up. If the tone is angry or punitive, then it's no longer a logical consequence.

* The same consequence can be respectful in one situation and demeaning in another. Mopping the floor is a respectful consequence for the child who chooses to have a water fight at the drinking fountain but not for the child who fails to complete his work.

Logical consequences are related to the child's behavior; punishment usually is not.

* Leaving the group is related to being disruptive in a group; missing recess is not. Cleaning up graffiti on the bathroom wall is related to drawing the graffiti on the walls; being suspended from school is not.

> Logical consequences respond to the misbehavior in ways that preserve the dignity of the child.

⁕ Logical consequences require that the teacher gather more information before reacting. The teacher takes time to assess the situation and determine, sometimes with input from the child, what will help fix the problem.

⁕ Here are a few questions teachers might ask themselves when trying to assess a situation:

What are the developmental issues at work here?

Is it clear to the child what is expected?

What rule is being broken?

What problem is the behavior creating?

What will help to solve the problem?

The belief underlying the use of logical consequences is that with reflection and practice children will want to do better, whereas the belief behind punishment is that children will do better only because they fear punishment and will seek to avoid it.

⁕ Teachers using logical consequences begin with a belief in the basic goodness of children and the knowledge that every child is a learner, struggling to establish meaningful relationships with us, each other, and the school community.

⁕ These teachers expect that all children will from time to time lose their controls and make mistakes.

⁕ The use of logical consequences helps children fix their mistakes and know what to do next time.

Teachers frequently ask, "Is it ever okay for children to feel bad about their behavior?" Of course it is. When children misbehave, chances are they already feel bad. Our job is not to make them feel worse but to help them choose a better course of action the next time.

As Ruth Sidney Charney says in *Teaching Children to Care*, "Our goal, when children break rules, is never to make them feel 'bad' or defeated, although they may, in fact, feel bad. Our goal is first to help them recover self-control and self-respect. When I observe a child acting the part of the bully, or sneaking out of a job, or putting down a classmate or teacher, it is not a picture of self-control and self-respect. It is a sign of distress and a signal for help. Something needs to stop. The use of logical consequences urges respect for the rules and the people they are designed to guide."

Building Empathy for a "Trouble Maker"

One Fifth-Sixth Grade Teacher's Experience

BY ALICE YANG

Chris was a student who struggled socially. He was in Sarah Fiarman's mixed-grade class for two years, first as a fifth grader and then as a sixth. Of all the points working against Chris, the biggest was probably his reputation as a trouble maker. By the time Chris came into Sarah's classroom as a fifth grader, most students in the school knew him as "mean" or "a bad kid" and were scared of him or disliked him. Sarah knew that if Chris was to become part of the classroom community, she would have to help the class and herself develop empathy for him and discover what Chris was really like behind the reputation.

"Building empathy for Chris was one of the most challenging experiences I've had as a teacher, but also one of the most rewarding," the Cambridge, Massachusetts, public school teacher says. Here are some strategies she found effective for working with Chris. Teachers may consider adapting these for use in similar teaching situations.

Avoid Connecting the Student's Name with Negatives

Sarah and her student teacher noticed that, almost as a rule, Chris's name was uttered, by children as well as teachers, in the same breath as a chastisement. "Chris, stop that!" "Chris, you're always cheating!" "You're doing it wrong, Chris!" It wasn't hard to imagine the damage to his image and self-image.

The teachers therefore made a conscious effort to avoid linking Chris's name with negatives. When they needed to redirect him, they would make general statements such as "Everyone needs to be looking at the board right now." "The other students wouldn't know whom I was speaking to, but Chris responded," says Sarah.

Know the Child before Drawing Conclusions

One day there arose a ruckus around the cricket cage. Chris was gripping the cage with both hands, shaking it hard. A crowd of classmates was screaming, "Stop it, Chris! Don't hurt the crickets!" After a moment, Chris calmly put the cage down and walked with a self-satisfied smirk through the crowd, much to his classmates' horror.

Sarah hurried over and asked, "What happened?" Accusations and defenses flew.

"Chris was trying to hurt the crickets!"

"I wasn't trying to hurt the crickets!"

"Yes, you were!"

"No, I wasn't!"

Seeing that this was going nowhere, Sarah calmed the children and brought the class together for a more structured conversation. However, Chris shut down and refused to respond when classmates expressed their concerns about the crickets.

The next day, Sarah called Chris to a private meeting with herself and the student teacher, Jons. In this less heated atmosphere, Chris admitted to shaking the crickets, but when Jons calmly asked why, it came out that the reason was not what everyone had assumed. "I thought they were dead," Chris explained. "They weren't moving. I was trying to see if they were still alive."

Indeed, as part of their science experiment, the children had put the crickets in the freezer to slow them down. Any child could easily have made the mistake of thinking they were dead.

"Looking back," says Sarah, "I realize that if I had observed Chris more closely during the times we worked with the crickets, I might have discovered for myself his genuine concern for the crickets and guessed his motivation for shaking them."

As for that smirk he wore as he walked through the crowd, Sarah learned later, after two years of observing Chris, that the look was his mechanism for protecting himself. "Chris was not a child who could articulate in the midst of conflict," she says. "His smirk and shut-down demeanor didn't mean he was cold or cruel. It meant he was trying to save face in the moment."

Use Real Classroom Moments to Build Compassion

Rather than talking with students about compassion in the abstract, Sarah believes it's more effective to use moments of conflict or awkwardness that naturally occur in the course of the day. In Sarah's class, snack time offered frequent opportunities for such real-life learning.

Each table of four students in the class shared a tray of snacks and had to decide how to divide up the food. "I knew this would bring Chris's social interaction issues to the forefront," says Sarah. "I knew it would provide opportunities for him and the other students to talk and listen to each other's feelings around sharing and being considerate of others."

To avoid setting Chris up for failure, however, Sarah had the class talk before starting the tray system. The children brainstormed ways in which tables could share the food, what might be hard, and possible ways to solve those problems.

But even with proactive work like this, students may still make mistakes, and Chris did. On the first day the class tried the tray system, Chris took a lot more than his share. The table erupted. "Chris! That's not fair! Put it back!" Chris responded just as sharply and continued taking.

99

Sarah recognized that giving Chris public responsibilities would be a way to improve his image and self-image.

Recognizing that Chris's mistake—any child's mistake—is an opportunity to learn, Sarah called Chris's table together. She told them they had to work out a better method for distributing the food. With some teacher guidance, the students were able to agree on an improved method. "I think this helped Chris realize that he had to be accountable to the group, even for a seemingly small thing like snack," Sarah says.

Later, the learning continued when Sarah brought the whole class together to talk about snack sharing, being careful not to use Chris's name, but to talk in general terms.

"Why do you think people might take more than their share?" she asked.

"Because they're selfish," students immediately answered.

"Okay. What are some other possible reasons?" Without discounting the "selfish" explanation, Sarah wanted to push the children to broaden their thinking.

After a pause, a few students offered other ideas:

"Maybe they're hungry."

"Maybe that's the way it worked in their old class."

"Maybe they're afraid other people might take more than their share, so they want to take a lot first."

Chris was silent through this conversation, but he was listening. He heard these motivations that he himself might have felt but couldn't articulate. He took in the way his peers showed compassion for someone in his situation, and therefore for him. "It was a powerful moment," says Sarah. "I could see the tension lift from him and sense his bad-boy reputation beginning to melt in the other children."

Give the Student Responsibilities Publicly

Sarah recognized that giving Chris public responsibilities would be a way to improve his image and self-image. For example, passing out the snack food to each table is a student job in Sarah's classroom. When she saw how much Chris enjoyed this job, she made him the "Snack Man" for the whole year.

Sarah also made Chris a public expert at things whenever possible. Chris happened to be a good speller. When a student asked, "How do I spell _____?" she'd often say, "Ask Chris. He's a walking dictionary."

Several things made this method successful. First, Sarah only gave Chris responsibilities he was ready for. That let him experience success and let his peers see him succeeding. Giving him responsibilities that were too big a stretch would have set him up for failure and risked reinforcing his negative image.

Second, Sarah used a matter-of-fact voice when referring other children to Chris. "If my tone had been gushy or even a bit over-enthusiastic, students would have felt manipulated," she explains.

Finally, when other students asked to help with a job of Chris's, such as passing out the food, Sarah always turned the question over to Chris. "Can Susan help out today?" This gave Chris the opportunity to welcome his peers and maintain real ownership of his responsibility. "Chris always—without exception—said yes, the classmate could help," Sarah recalls. "I think he appreciated being given the choice. He was learning the habit of including others and, I think, even took pride in it."

The Power of Creating a Safe Space

Sarah had high expectations for Chris's behavior and he responded. But just as important as the teacher's expectations was how Chris's peers perceived him. By sending the other students a message early on that Chris was a valuable member of the class, the teacher helped shape their interactions and expectations of him. "Together, we created a space where Chris could gradually let down his guard and be the great kid he really is," says Sarah.

101

Teacher-Child Problem-Solving Conferences

Involving Children in Finding Solutions to Their Behavior Problems

AN ADAPTED EXCERPT FROM THE NEFC BOOK *TEACHING CHILDREN TO CARE* BY RUTH SIDNEY CHARNEY

Derek was a fifth grader who was avoiding writing. Whenever we had writing time, he would ask to go to the bathroom, and there he would linger. After observing this for a week, I decided to have a problem-solving conference with him.

A problem-solving conference is a technique for addressing a specific problem that a child is having. What makes it powerful is that it invites the child into a conversation and asks for the child's take on the situation.

The conference begins with the teacher noticing the child's moods, actions, and interactions before helping the child come up with possible solutions. Conducted in a nonjudgmental way, the conference sets behavioral boundaries while giving children the opportunity for autonomous thinking.

In this article, I'll describe the basic steps that I went through in the conference with Derek. These steps are intended as guidelines to be adjusted to fit different situations. Some conferences take five minutes; others are spread out over several days. In some cases a conference leads to an immediate solution; in others the teacher and child need to revisit the issue several times.

One thing that is true of all problem-solving conferences, though, is that I always hold them away from the eyes and ears of the child's classmates. It's important that the student has privacy for these talks, and that the teacher and child can both focus on the conversation without interruptions.

Step 1. Establishing What the Teacher and Student Notice

A problem-solving conference begins with the teacher saying positive things she or he has noticed about the student—the student's interests, efforts, and goings-on. When we tell students we noticed what they've done well, we begin to establish a supportive connection, an essential step before talking about a behavior that isn't working.

With Derek, I began by saying, "I notice that you've had good ideas when we've brainstormed what we could write about. I also notice you pay attention and make helpful comments when kids share about their writing." I try to be specific in my noticings, and I name the "what," not the "why," of behaviors.

Next I say what behavior I've noticed that isn't working well. Here again, it's important to name specific, observable behaviors. I don't make judgments, interpret, or label. I simply describe, using a matter-of-fact tone.

"I notice that every writing time, you have to go to the bathroom," I said to Derek. I was careful not to say, "You want to avoid writing, so you say you have to go to the bathroom."

By naming the behaviors rather than interpreting them, I open the door for children to take note of their actions and offer their own interpretation. They are then more likely to take responsibility for their behavior.

After I say what I notice, I ask for the child's observations. I say simply "What do you notice?" in a neutral tone.

When I posed this question to Derek, he said, "I just have to go to the bathroom a lot."

"So you also notice that writing has become a bathroom time for you?"

"Yeah."

Derek was agreeing with my observation. If he had disagreed, I might have said, "Well, I notice that you want to go to the bathroom at every writing time. You notice that it's only sometimes. Maybe we should both notice extra hard for the next few days and then come back and compare." I would have made a plan with Derek for how to remember our observations. But I also would have continued with the conference. It's possible to proceed in addressing a problem while we continue to gather data.

Step 2. Naming the Problem and the Need to Solve It

The next step is to help the child see why her or his behavior is a problem and to establish that the child wants to work with the teacher to solve it.

To Derek I said, "When you go to the bathroom every writing period, you lose important work time. By the time you get back, you have to hurry and often you only get about a sentence written."

"Yeah. There's not enough time."

"So your story doesn't get very far. For example, you don't have very much yet of the story you're writing now."

"Yeah. I only have the first page."

"I want you to be able to write complete stories that you can be proud of. So this seems like a problem we should work on. What do you think?"

"I guess so."

Here it's important for the teacher to express positive intent—for the student to get along with others, have friends, enjoy and take pride in his or her work, solve math word problems, or follow directions—and to show faith that the child will make progress.

Sometimes when we ask whether a child wants to work with us on the problem, we get only a slight nod or other gesture of agreement—which is fine. We go ahead.

Other times, a child refuses adamantly: "No, I don't need help!" or "No, I don't think it's a problem." If this happens, it might be useless to push ahead with the conference.

However, it's important that I state the expectations for behavior—for example, for the child to stop putting others down, to get work done, or to end aggressive behavior. I might say, "I see that it's hard to discuss this right now. I'd like to help. Let's see if the rude comments stop."

We gain children's confidence when we invite them to participate in the conversation.

Step 3. Understanding the Cause of the Problem

When the student and I agree that there's a problem (even if there's only a moderate or muffled agreement from the student) and we agree there's a need to solve it, we explore the "why" behind the problem. I suggest possible causes based on an understanding of children's need to belong, feel competent, and have choices. I'm also aware that confusion or frustration about academics may be an underlying cause. I often use "Could it be …" questions to initiate this discussion.

To Derek I said, "When I see kids go to the bathroom at a particular time every day, I think they want to avoid something they don't like or that's hard for them. Could it be that writing seems hard for you this year?"

Derek grinned and said, "Sort of. It's sort of hard."

Children don't always give a clear answer to our "Could it be …" questions. A "yeah, maybe," a slight nod, or sometimes a "yes" disguised as a shoulder shrug may be all we get. But those signals let us know it's okay to go on.

With Derek, I probed further to get at why writing was hard for him. As happens with many children, I needed to name several possible causes before he heard one that sounded right. "Could it be that writing is hard because you have trouble thinking of ideas? Or could it be that you know your main ideas, but you get confused about what words to use? Sometimes writers worry about the spelling or the handwriting. Could that be true for you?"

"Sometimes I can't think of the words I want," Derek replied.

Even when the cause of the behavior is very clear to me, I ask rather than assert. We gain children's confidence when we invite them to participate in the conversation. This confidence grows not because the teacher has brilliantly solved the mystery, but because the child was part of the process.

Step 4. Generating Alternatives

"Do you think we could come up with some ways to help you remember the words you need?" I said next to Derek.

It often helps to list several alternatives before seizing upon one solution. In Derek's case, we decided together that he could brainstorm a list of words before starting a story. He could try some story mapping exercises. Or he could jot down main ideas before starting to write.

Step 5. Choosing One Strategy to Try

The conference ends with an oral or written agreement to try one of the alternatives. With several possible strategies on the table, I asked Derek to choose one idea to try. He chose to try brainstorming a list of words.

Always, it's important that students choose an alternative that they believe will work, not one that just pleases the teacher. Over the next days and weeks, the student and teacher both take note of whether the problem they identified gets resolved. If not, they learn from the experience and return to the list of alternatives to make a better selection.

The strength of this problem-solving approach is its openness to the child's perspective and ideas. We try to see children as they really are, exploring with them what they need in order to do better at school. Ironically the correct solution is not what's most important. What's most important is inviting the child into the conversation, searching together for solutions, and expressing faith in the child's ability to solve the problem.

Beyond Coping

Helping a Child Who Struggles with Anger

BY CAROLYN BUSH

When Corey joined my fourth grade class, he already had a history of school struggles and had spent part of third grade in a self-contained room for children with behavior problems. When he was mainstreamed into my class in fourth grade, Corey had trouble making good choices, interacting with others, and following directions. He was often angry, and managing his unpredictable outbursts required a great deal of attention from me and other adults at school.

Our strategies for that year focused primarily on controlling Corey's behavior in order to preserve a safe, calm learning environment. Often the quickest way to achieve this involved removing Corey. For example, rather than risk having Corey line up with the other children after recess (when someone always "looked at him wrong"), I'd have him deliver a note to the office and then meet us back at the classroom.

This way of coping averted many meltdowns, but it was a lot of work for the adults involved, emphasized differences between Corey and the other children, and did little to help Corey develop the self-management skills he lacked. So when I

> Corey, like all children, needed to feel he belonged before he could feel motivated to learn and grow.

learned I'd be teaching the same children as fifth graders again the next year, I decided that a new approach was in order.

Getting Ready

Before school started, I read books, talked to colleagues, and reflected on my beliefs about children and teaching to see what I might do differently this time around. One result of this process was that I set two specific goals for the coming year: to make the classroom a safer and more rewarding place of learning for all the children, and to help Corey begin learning to manage his own behavior.

With those goals in mind and the support of the school community, I found many opportunities to change my approach. This article describes just a few of these strategies.

Beginning with Belonging

The first change was a deliberate shift in how we viewed Corey as a member of the class. When I reflected on the previous year, I saw that belonging to our classroom community had been considered a privilege for Corey, something he could lose by misbehaving. In fact, if he lost control too many times, he'd be removed from the class permanently, as he had been in third grade. As a result, going to time-out or the reflection room had a different meaning for Corey than for the other children in the class. The others could use disciplinary time away from the class as it was intended—as a chance to regain their self-control, knowing they would be welcomed back when they were ready. For Corey, every incident felt as if he'd earned another strike in a game in which he didn't know how many strikes he was allowed before he struck out.

This system was particularly unfair to Corey because he lacked the skills he needed to control his behavior. So failure was all he knew, when what he needed was to experience success and gradual improvement. We had to find ways to teach him positive behavior skills, build up his confidence, and show him that although there were consequences for unacceptable behavior, he'd be forgiven for his mistakes.

Therefore, Corey's fifth grade year began with a clear statement to him, his family, and all the adults who worked with him at school: Corey belonged in our class, not on a trial basis, and not only if he controlled himself. If he lost control, he still might need to leave the room for a while. The difference now, however, was that we'd expect him to return and allow him to start over with a clean slate. This was a crucial first step. Corey, like all children, needed to feel he belonged before he could feel motivated to learn and grow.

Revising Corey's Behavior Contract

We also revised the behavior contract that had been developed for Corey

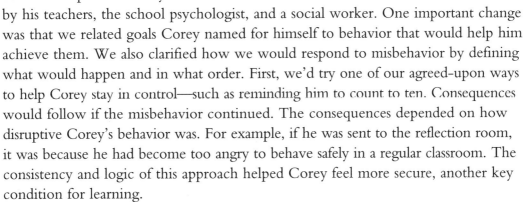

Learn More

For more information on working with children with challenging behaviors, see:

The Explosive Child by Ross Greene. HarperCollins. 2005. Available at www.responsiveclassroom.org/book store/rp_explosivechild.html.

Positive Discipline by Jane Nelsen. Ballantine Books. 2006. Available at www.responsiveclassroom.org/ bookstore/rp_positivediscipline.html.

"Positive Time-Out" by NEFC Staff. Winter 2004. www.responsiveclassroom.org/newsletter/16_1nl_1. html.

"Buddy Teachers: Lending a hand to keep time-out positive and productive" by Alice Yang and Ruth Sidney Charney. Winter 2005. www.responsiveclass room.org/newsletter/17_1nl_1.html.

"Refusing to Go to Time-Out" by Ruth Sidney Charney. April 2002. www.responsiveclassroom.org/pdf_files/ qa_10.pdf

"Getting Past 'I Can't'" from Andy Dousis as told to Roxann Kriete. February 2008. www.responsiveclass room.org/ newsletter/20_1nl_1.html.

by his teachers, the school psychologist, and a social worker. One important change was that we related goals Corey named for himself to behavior that would help him achieve them. We also clarified how we would respond to misbehavior by defining what would happen and in what order. First, we'd try one of our agreed-upon ways to help Corey stay in control—such as reminding him to count to ten. Consequences would follow if the misbehavior continued. The consequences depended on how disruptive Corey's behavior was. For example, if he was sent to the reflection room, it was because he had become too angry to behave safely in a regular classroom. The consistency and logic of this approach helped Corey feel more secure, another key condition for learning.

Working One-on-One

With Corey, I focused on building his repertoire of anger management skills. For example, in his behavior contract he agreed that "if I am angry I will go to the person in charge." That way, an adult could remind him of the techniques he'd learned for calming himself down and possibly avert an explosion. Since this was a new behavior for Corey, he needed support while he learned. One way I helped was to check in with him regularly, often at the beginning of the day. During these brief meetings, we'd rehearse appropriate ways he could let me know he needed my attention, such as using eye contact, gestures, and calm words. We also practiced similar signals that I would use to show him that I was aware he was upset and wanted to help.

Involving the Class

Meanwhile, the whole class worked on dealing with anger, a skill I believe is important for all children to develop. We talked about what anger felt like to each of us, and how we could tell when someone else was starting to feel angry. We practiced strategies such as counting to ten and "taking a quiet moment" to collect our thoughts when things weren't going well. We also considered what we could do to help someone who was feeling angry, including moving quietly and calmly away from a tense situation. We practiced all these skills in noncrisis situations so we'd be comfortable using them when things heated up.

This work helped the class feel more competent. It also helped the children feel more confident in the face of Corey's anger. Some were even able to help. When Corey would clench his fists or set his jaw, some boys discovered that they could be his champions, calmly reminding him of ways he might regain control by asking "Hey man, do you need to cool down?" or suggesting that he "take five." Other children helped by getting out of the way so I could reach Corey quickly when he started to tense up. As we learned to recognize signs of problems brewing and started intervening more quickly, the number of full-blown incidents decreased.

Reflecting on My Own

One of the most powerful strategies I tried was making reflection a part of my routine. One technique that worked well was keeping a journal. During an incident, I'd focus on defusing the situation, but afterwards, as soon as I could be alone (usually when the class was at lunch or a special), I'd get out my notebook and pour all that I remembered onto the pages. I didn't worry about whether my words made sense. I just jotted down as much as I could, put the journal away, and went on with the day. Although it was sometimes hard to take the time to do this writing, I usually felt better afterwards.

After school, when I was feeling calm, I'd sit with a cup of cocoa and review what I'd written. That's when things would begin to make sense. Re-reading helped me see what was really happening and plan ways to follow up. For instance, I began to see a pattern in Corey's behavior: When he began complaining about physical aches and pains, the next few days would be difficult. I used this knowledge to alert Corey's other teachers and also made sure to check in with him on those days.

One of the most powerful strategies I tried was making reflection a part of my routine.

I also rehearsed ways to stay calm and focused on my goals in those heated moments. When I re-read what I wrote about my reactions to Corey's actions, I saw how responding angrily only made things worse. In my journal I reminded myself that I didn't need to take Corey's behavior personally and encouraged myself to take a few moments to think before acting. In those few seconds, I could make choices, including the choice to remove my anger from the situation and respond calmly. Over time, although my buttons still got pushed, there were fewer instances when I lost my temper.

A More Peaceable Community

With the help of many others in our school community, Corey, his classmates, and I made some real progress during that school year. Slowly, Corey became more skillful at managing his anger, all the children learned techniques that made them more caring and competent, and I worked out some new ways to help children like Corey. Best of all, I enjoyed this class as fifth graders so much! I could never have guessed how far we'd travel on our two-year journey toward becoming a more peaceable community.

What Teaching Matthew Taught Me

FROM ANDY DOUSIS AS TOLD TO ROXANN KRIETE

"Matthew! Get away. You're not sitting with us!" Libby hissed the words, her voice oozing with contempt as she stuck her leg out to keep Matthew from joining the small group gathered for silent reading.

I whipped around. The vehemence in Libby's voice shocked me. Libby generally treated her classmates with kindness and seldom spoke sharply to anyone.

Disturbed by this exchange, I observed the interactions between Matthew and his classmates closely for the remainder of that mid-December day. I did not like what I saw and heard. At midday outside, Matthew was standing by the wall, crying. When I asked what was wrong, he replied through sniffles, "The boys won't let me play. They said I'm not good enough." After I spoke with the students he meant, they called for Matthew to join their Four Square game, but he no longer wanted to.

Later in the afternoon, when Matthew returned from his visit with a reading teacher, he approached a group of children and asked to join their activity. "No, we've already started," one child said in an unfriendly tone. The child's words were not the issue. It was her tone.

There were several more instances of children speaking sharply and negatively to Matthew.

I left school that day feeling discouraged. From the first day of school I had worked hard to help the students build a caring classroom community. I had seen it taking hold, but it sure was not flourishing today. What was going on?

Not an Easy Child to Be Around

When did the students' treatment of Matthew erode? What brought it on? And why had I not noticed?

Puzzling through this, I reminded myself that I had known all along that making Matthew a full member of the classroom community would be an uphill climb, for Matthew was not an easy child to be around. He had entered fourth grade saddled with more challenges than any one child should have to bear. He often came to school unwashed and in ill-fitting clothes. His shirt never covered his big belly; his pants never reached his ankles. He struggled with academics, barely reading at first grade level. He dissolved into loud sobs at the least frustration. Finding the right words to make his way into a conversation or to ask for something was a struggle. So Matthew frequently poked and pushed and grabbed. His chronic outbursts wore his classmates—and teachers—out.

Before school had even started, I knew that I would have to work especially hard to make sure Matthew had a respected place in the room. I called on him for answers when I knew he had them. I partnered him with students who could be counted on to work patiently with him. In the first few months things seemed to go pretty well. Matthew was at least tolerated and well-treated, if not yet a cherished class member. Not so today. When did the students' treatment of Matthew erode? What brought it on? And why had I not noticed?

Turning My Observer's Eye Upon Myself

My inner voice said that if I wanted the answers, I had to first look at myself. Over the years I've learned that good teaching involves having a willingness to look

I decided that I needed to see Matthew with new eyes, to look again for the positives in Matthew.

at your own behavior and ask what part you might be playing in what's going on in your classroom—the good and the not-so-good. So the next day I turned my observer's eye upon myself and began to note my own behavior. Before Morning Meeting started, Matthew was butting his head into Tyler's shoulder. "Matthew! Stop!" I snapped. As students moved from Morning Meeting into math groups, I heard myself barking, "Matthew! Sit down now!" I seemed unable to speak the child's name without an exclamation point behind it.

I reflected. In September I would have redirected Matthew with a gentle hand on his shoulder or a quiet "Matt, move over here now." In September I made sure to welcome him warmly at the beginning of each day. Today I did not check in with him before Morning Meeting. In September I made it a point to use Matthew's name in positive comments. Today I was loudly and frequently calling attention to his awkwardness.

I realized how very tired I was. Tired from the intense energy that the first phase of the school year requires and hungry for the late December week off that marked the first substantial break of the year. In addition to this predictable energy dip, the effort required to help the intensely needy Matt navigate daily classroom life added to my fatigue. As my exhaustion grew, my alertness to our classroom interactions diminished. I managed to overlook the rough tones and edgy words creeping into the children's—and my—interactions with Matthew until they had escalated to an undeniably attention-grabbing level.

But now I was noticing. Moreover, as I continued to notice, it became clear that I was contributing to Matthew's mistreatment. But wait, let me be more precise: I wasn't just contributing to his mistreatment. I was teaching it. When I snapped at him, I gave permission to twenty-three others to snap at him, too. I was using a surefire teaching strategy: modeling. I knew well the power of modeling and used it often and intentionally: "Watch how I lift Matilda out of her cage." "Watch while I dribble the soccer ball around Jen." "What did you notice? Now you try it this way."

I realized that my interactions with Matthew were a powerful, unintentional modeling. When I stopped seeking Matthew out to say a friendly hello in the

morning, the students stopped,
too. When I snapped commands at him, they snapped, too. I was
treated to a painful refresher lesson about the strength of modeling.

Determined to Turn Things Around

Having seen and acknowledged my role in what was going awry, I needed to make some changes. It wasn't easy, given how tired I was. But my determination was greater than my fatigue. I decided that I needed to see Matthew with new eyes, to look again for the positives in Matthew. And then, through intentional modeling, I needed to help the class see the positives in him as well. I found five specific ways to do this:

I did everything possible to use words and tone with Matthew masterfully. There was no room for slippage with him. I would call him "Matt," his preferred nickname. I would speak quietly.

I looked for—and publicized—instances of positive behavior from Matthew. This was tougher than it might sound, because the things I noted had to be real. Students can spot any phoniness right away. But I was able to see real positive efforts on Matthew's part when I worked at it—every single day. And it got easier. The more I watched, the more I noted how hard Matthew was working. And the more I noted, the harder he worked.

I sought help from the whole staff. I asked the principal if I could bring my struggle to our faculty meeting. "I've screwed up," I stated to the group, "and I need your help." I asked everyone to be especially patient and positive with Matthew so that he would receive consistent treatment from us all. Every colleague agreed to help.

I looked for some area in which Matthew could be the class expert. I found it quite by luck. One day I brought in several discarded appliances gathered from friends—an iron, a couple of hair driers, an old-fashioned alarm clock—and created a Take-It-Apart station in the room.

It turned out that Matthew excelled in this area. He could take apart virtually anything and reassemble it. A pile of screws and odd-shaped metal objects that left his classmates baffled were an engrossing 3-D jigsaw for Matthew. I added more and more complex objects as the weeks went by, and I put Matthew in charge of the area. Students would come to me for help, and I'd furrow my brow, shrug, and say, "Ask Matt." And ask Matt they did. "Thanks, Matt," I began to hear routinely when I walked by the Take-It-Apart station.

115

I made sure the class also saw Matthew being competent in learning academics. This was challenging not just because of his beginning reading skills, but also because of his limited participation in the class's academic program due to being pulled out often for intensive academic support. But remembering that he had once talked with some excitement about a TV show on wolves, I suggested that he learn more about them.

With help from his special education teacher, Matthew researched the topic, relying on videos and magazine articles with lots of pictures and captions, and planned a presentation to the class. He worked hard on an accurate drawing of a wolf with painstaking labeling. He created a set of posters with pertinent vocabulary words: endangered, predator, carnivore, hunter. He drew a map to depict where North American wolves live. He practiced his presentation in the resource room. On the day of the presentation to our class, his parents came in for the occasion. School was clearly not a comfortable place for them, but they were there, and they were proud.

I can still hear Matthew's high-pitched voice and see him rocking back and forth, heels-to-toes-to-heels as he began, "I'm gonna talk about wolves. First I'm gonna show a little bit of a video … " His presentation was well received. The class was genuinely interested and their questions were many and real. "Where do red wolves live?" "Are there wolves around here?" "How much does a wolf weigh?" "Why are wolves endangered?" Matthew had an answer for every question. He had acquired another area of expertise. In small, solid increments, Matthew's classroom currency was growing.

A Lesson That Served Me Very Well

The rest of the year had its ups and downs, but it's safe to say that it was a good year for Matthew and for the rest of the class. Although he didn't have friends in the typical ten-year-old way, he had a respected place in the class. One colleague who knew Matthew came up to me one day in the spring and said, "You know, I think this is the best year that Matthew's ever had."

As I followed Matthew through the subsequent years, I was pleased to see him make continued progress. His path was not an easy one, but I think the lessons he learned in fourth grade served him well. I know that what I learned about teaching—courtesy of Matthew—has served me well in all the years since.

RECOMMENDED RESOURCES

For more information about the ideas and practices discussed in the articles in this book, and for general information about the *Responsive Classroom*® approach, see the resources listed below. To order any of these resources, go to the *Responsive Classroom* website, www.responsiveclassroom.org.

Academic Choice

Learning Through Academic Choice. Paula Denton. Turners Falls, Massachusetts: Northeast Foundation for Children, Inc. 2005.

Challenging Behaviors

The Explosive Child: A New Approach for Understanding and Parenting Easily Frustrated, Chronically Inflexible Children. Ross W. Greene. New York: HarperCollins. 2001.

The Respectful School: How Educators and Students Can Conquer Hate and Harassment. Stephen L. Wessler. Alexandria, Virginia: Association for Supervision and Curriculum Development. 2003.

Child Development

Child Development Pamphlet Series. Content adapted from *Yardsticks: Children in the Classroom Ages 4–14*. Turners Falls, Massachusetts: Northeast Foundation for Children, Inc. 2005.

Yardsticks: Children in the Classroom Ages 4–14. Third edition. Chip Wood. Turners Falls, Massachusetts: Northeast Foundation for Children, Inc. 2007.

Classroom Management

Positive Discipline. Revised edition. Jane Nelsen. New York: Ballantine Books. 2006.

Teaching Children to Care: Classroom Management for Ethical and Academic Growth, K–8. Ruth Sidney Charney. Turners Falls, Massachusetts: Northeast Foundation for Children, Inc. 2002.

Classroom Organization

Classroom Spaces That Work. Marlynn K. Clayton with Mary Beth Forton. Turners Falls, Massachusetts: Northeast Foundation for Children, Inc. 2001.

First Six Weeks of School

The First Day of School in a Responsive Classroom (40-minute DVD). Turners Falls, Massachusetts: Northeast Foundation for Children, Inc. 2007.

The First Six Weeks of School. Paula Denton and Roxann Kriete. Turners Falls, Massachusetts: Northeast Foundation for Children, Inc. 2000.

Morning Meeting

99 Activities and Greetings: Great for Morning Meeting and other meetings, too! Melissa Correa-Connolly. Turners Falls, Massachusetts: Northeast Foundation for Children, Inc. 2004.

Doing Morning Meeting: The Essential Components (30-minute DVD). Turners Falls, Massachusetts and Portland, Maine: Northeast Foundation for Children, Inc., and Stenhouse Publishers. 2004.

The Morning Meeting Book. Roxann Kriete with contributions by Lynn Bechtel. Turners Falls, Massachusetts: Northeast Foundation for Children, Inc. 1999.

Morning Meeting Messages K–6: 180 Sample Charts from Three Classrooms. Rosalea S. Fisher, Eric Henry, and Deborah Porter. Turners Falls, Massachusetts: Northeast Foundation for Children, Inc. 2006.

Parent–Teacher Collaboration

Parents & Teachers Working Together. Carol Davis and Alice Yang. Turners Falls, Massachusetts: Northeast Foundation for Children, Inc. 2005.

Rules and Logical Consequences

Creating Rules with Students in a Responsive Classroom (35-minute DVD). Turners Falls, Massachusetts: Northeast Foundation for Children, Inc. 2007.

Rules in School. Kathryn Brady, Mary Beth Forton, Deborah Porter, and Chip Wood. Turners Falls, Massachusetts: Northeast Foundation for Children, Inc. 2003.

Time-Out in a Responsive Classroom (35-minute DVD). Turners Falls, Massachusetts: Northeast Foundation for Children, Inc. 2007.

Schedule and Pacing of School

Time to Teach, Time to Learn. Chip Wood. Turners Falls, Massachusetts: Northeast Foundation for Children, Inc. 1999.

Schoolwide Community

In Our School: Building Community in Elementary Schools. Karen L. Casto and Jennifer R. Audley. Turners Falls, Massachusetts: Northeast Foundation for Children, Inc. 2008.

Song, Movement, and Games

16 Songs Kids Love to Sing (CD and book). Turners Falls, Massachusetts: Northeast Foundation for Children, Inc. 1998.

36 Games Kids Love to Play. Adrian Harrison. Turners Falls, Massachusetts: Northeast Foundation for Children, Inc. 2002.

85 Engaging Movement Activities. Phyllis S. Weikart and Elizabeth B. Carlton. Ypsilanti, Michigan: High/Scope Press. 2002.

Down in the Valley: More Great Singing Games for Children (CD and book). Brattleboro, Vermont: New England Dancing Masters. 2000.

Teacher Language

Choice Words: How Our Language Affects Children's Learning. Peter H. Johnston. Portland, Maine: Stenhouse Publishers. 2004.

How to Talk So Kids Can Learn at Home and in School. Adele Faber and Elaine Mazlish. New York: Simon and Schuster. 1995.

The Power of Our Words: Teacher Language That Helps Children Learn. Paula Denton. Turners Falls, Massachusetts: Northeast Foundation for Children, Inc. 2007.

Jennifer R. Audley is managing editor of the *Responsive Classroom® Newsletter* and website at NEFC. She has experience as a classroom teacher, researcher, editor, and educational consultant. She is the co-author of *In Our School: Building Community in Elementary Schools*.

Carolyn Bush, now in her eleventh year of teaching, has taught second, fourth, and fifth grades, all at K.T. Murphy Elementary School in Stamford, Connecticut. Carolyn is a *Responsive Classroom* consulting teacher and a certified teacher mentor for the Stamford public schools.

Karen L. Casto has taught middle school, high school, and college and was a middle and high school administrator before becoming principal of Penn Valley Elementary School in Levittown, Pennsylvania, a role she held for nine years. She is a consulting administrator for NEFC. Karen is the co-author of *In Our School: Building Community in Elementary Schools*.

Ruth Sidney Charney, a co-founder of NEFC, has been teaching children and adults for over thirty-five years. Her career has included teaching kindergarten through eighth grade, presenting teacher workshops, and consulting in schools. Ruth is the author of *Teaching Children to Care: Classroom Management for Ethical and Academic Growth, K–8*.

Marlynn K. Clayton has twenty years of experience as a classroom teacher in the primary grades. A co-founder of NEFC, she has devoted years to helping teachers implement the *Responsive Classroom* approach through giving workshops, providing coaching, and writing books and articles. Marlynn is the author of *Classroom Spaces That Work*.

Caltha Crowe taught preschool and elementary children during her thirty-five-year education career. Her most recent experience was in teaching third graders at Kings Highway School in Westport, Connecticut, where she also served as a mentor for new teachers. Caltha is a frequent presenter of *Responsive Classroom* workshops for NEFC and also serves on the NEFC Board of Directors.

Carol Davis has worked as an elementary school teacher and counselor in Ohio and Washington, DC. She is an experienced presenter of *Responsive Classroom* workshops and is the co-author of *Parents and Teachers Working Together*.

Paula Denton has taught since 1985 and has been a *Responsive Classroom* consulting teacher since 1990. She is currently director of program development and delivery for NEFC. Paula is the author of *Learning Through Academic Choice* and *The Power of Our Words: Teacher Language That Helps Children Learn* and co-author of *The First Six Weeks of School*.

Andy Dousis is an on-staff senior consulting teacher at NEFC. Before joining NEFC he taught third and fourth graders for ten years at Flanders Elementary School in East Lyme, Connecticut, and presented *Responsive Classroom* workshops for NEFC. He is the co-author of *The Research-Ready Classroom: Differentiating Instruction Across Content Areas*.

Megan Earls has been teaching in New York City public schools for eight years. She has taught fourth, fifth, and sixth grades, and served as founding English teacher for Williamsburg Collegiate, a pubic charter school in Brooklyn.

Mark Farnsworth began teaching elementary school physical education in 1993. During his education career he has also served as an administrator and sports coach. Mark is a *Responsive Classroom* consulting teacher and presents workshops on applying the approach to the playground and PE settings.

Sarah Fiarman, a National Board certified teacher, taught grades three through six at the Cambridgeport School in Cambridge, Massachusetts. She is a *Responsive Classroom* consulting teacher. Currently Sarah is on leave from classroom teaching to pursue a doctoral degree from Harvard's Graduate School of Education.

Mary Beth Forton is the director of publications for NEFC. Before embarking on a career in publications, she taught language arts in elementary and middle schools, specializing in working with students with learning difficulties. She is a co-author of *Rules in School*.

Gail Healy has been the principal of Four Corners Elementary School in Greenfield, Massachusetts, for fourteen years. Under Gail's leadership and with a dynamic group of teachers, Four Corners has implemented the *Responsive Classroom* approach for over ten years and hosts visits by many school teams who want to observe the approach in action. In 2007 Four Corners received a Compass School award from the state of Massachusetts for above-target academic achievement.

Nancy Kovacic began her career in preK–8 education in 1967. She taught third grade for seventeen years at Coleytown Elementary in Westport, Connecticut, before becoming a math support teacher for grades 1-5 at Kings Highway School in Westport. A long-time *Responsive Classroom* practitioner, she has been providing training in the approach in her district for six years.

Roxann Kriete is the executive director of NEFC. She began her work at NEFC in 1985 as a teacher of grades five through eight. She is a co-author of *The First Six Weeks of School* and the author of *The Morning Meeting Book*.

Jay Lord, an NEFC co-founder, has taught middle school grades, high school, and college in urban and rural U.S. settings as well as overseas during his lifelong career in education. At NEFC, he has served as teacher, workshop presenter, executive director, and business manager. He is now NEFC's director of marketing.

Margaret Berry Wilson is a professional development specialist at NEFC. Before joining NEFC, she taught for fourteen years—as a first and second grade teacher in Nashville, Tennessee, and then as a kindergarten teacher in San Bernardino, California.

Chip Wood, an NEFC co-founder, has worked with children from preschool through eighth grade as a classroom teacher, teaching principal, and teacher educator. Author of *Yardsticks: Children in the Classroom Ages 4–14*, Chip has made developmentally based teaching the center of his educational practice. Chip is currently principal of Sheffield Elementary School in Turners Falls, Massachusetts.

Alice Yang has been in the writing and editing field for over twenty years. She joined NEFC in 2000 and has served as writer/editor, manager of publications, and senior editor. She is a co-author of *Parents and Teachers Working Together*.

ABOUT THE *RESPONSIVE CLASSROOM* APPROACH

The *Responsive Classroom* approach to teaching emphasizes social, emotional, and academic growth in a strong and safe school community. The goal is to enable optimal student learning. Created by classroom teachers and backed by evidence from independent research, the *Responsive Classroom* approach consists of classroom and schoolwide practices for deliberately helping children build academic and social-emotional competencies.

At the heart of the *Responsive Classroom* approach are ten classroom practices:

Morning Meeting—gathering as a class each morning to greet each other and warm up for the day ahead

Rule Creation—helping students create classroom rules that allow all class members to meet learning goals

Interactive Modeling—teaching children expected behaviors through a unique modeling technique

Positive Teacher Language—using words and tone in ways that promote children's active learning and self-discipline

Logical Consequences—responding to misbehavior in a way that allows children to fix and learn from their mistakes while preserving their dignity

Guided Discovery—introducing classroom materials using a format that encourages independence, creativity, and responsibility

Academic Choice—increasing student motivation and learning by allowing students teacher-structured choices in their work

Classroom Organization—setting up the physical room in ways that encourage students' independence, cooperation, and productivity

Working with Families—involving them as partners and helping them understand the school's teaching approaches

Collaborative Problem-Solving—using conferencing, role-playing, and other strategies to resolve problems with students

More information about the *Responsive Classroom*
approach is available through:

Publications and Resources

❋ Books and videos for elementary school educators

❋ Free quarterly newsletter for elementary educators

❋ Website offering articles and other information:
www.responsiveclassroom.org

Professional Development Opportunities

❋ One-day and week-long workshops for teachers

❋ One-day workshops for administrators

❋ Classroom consultations and other services at individual schools and districts

❋ Annual conference for school leaders

For details, contact:

Northeast Foundation for Children, Inc.
85 Avenue A, Suite 204, P.O. Box 718
Turners Falls, MA 01376-0718

800-360-6332   FAX: 877-206-3952
www.responsiveclassroom.org